Intermediate

GLOBAL GATE

— Video-based Four Skills Training —

Azusa Wada Bill Benfield Akira Morita

photographs by

iStockphoto / Shutterstock / Getty Images / 時事 / EPA＝時事 / AFP＝時事

時事通信フォト / Lehtikuva/時事通信フォト / GRANGER/時事通信フォト

videos by

Ready to Run

StreamLine

Web 動画・音声ファイルのストリーミング再生について

CD マーク及び Web 動画マークがある箇所は、PC、スマートフォン、タブレット端末において、無料でストリーミング再生することができます。下記 URL よりご利用ください。再生手順や動作環境などは本書巻末の「Web 動画のご案内」をご覧ください。

https://st.seibido.co.jp

音声ファイルのダウンロードについて

CD マークがある箇所は、ダウンロードすることも可能です。下記 URL の書籍詳細ページにあるダウンロードアイコンをクリックしてください。

https://www.seibido.co.jp/ad686

Global Gate Intermediate

CONTENTS

LEARNING OVERVIEW

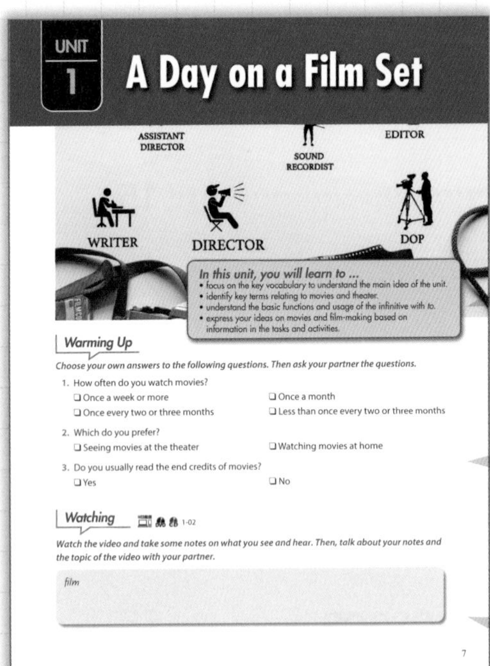

In this unit, you will learn to ...

An overview of the unit helps students focus on learning outcomes.

Warming Up

Activates students' background knowledge of the topic.

Watching

Presents a video for students to watch and recognize key words or phrases.

Vocabulary

Teaches the definitions and usage of topic-related words or phrases.

Tips on Listening and Speaking

Presents useful information for listening and speaking.

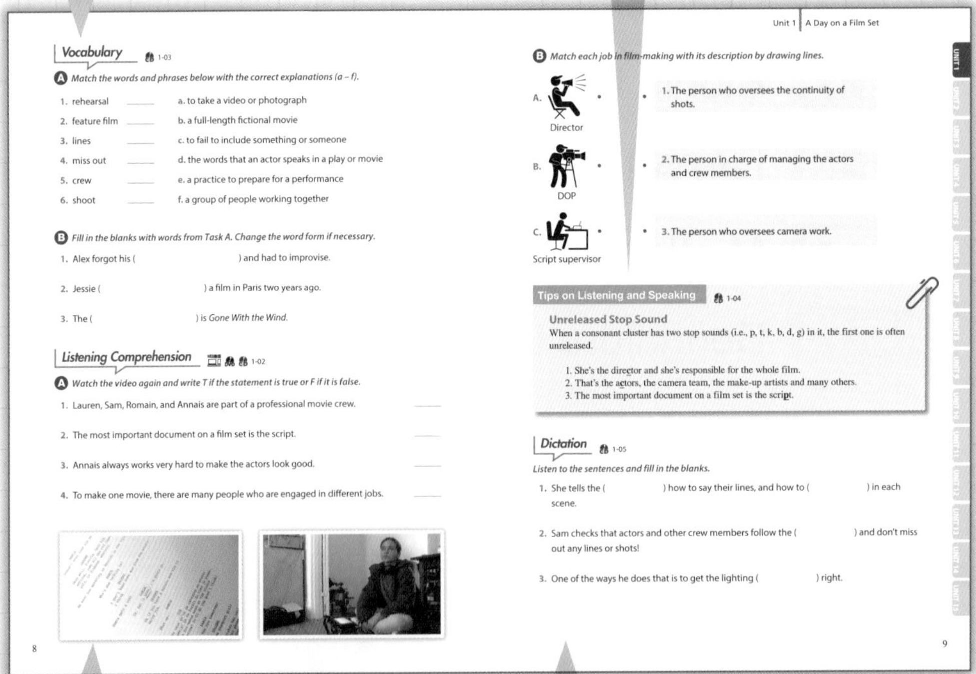

Listening Comprehension

Presents various review questions for students to check comprehension.

Dictation

Teaches sound features related to Tips on Listening and Speaking as well as content words from the video.

Retelling

Presents parts of the video for students to watch and retell in their own words.

Grammar

Presents a thorough explanation of the grammar point of the unit.

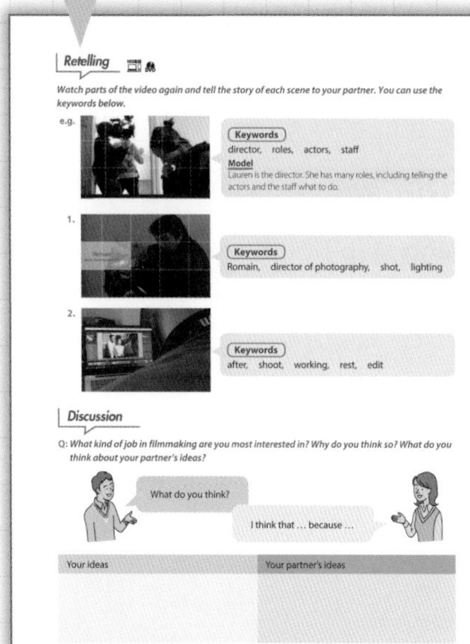

Retelling

Watch parts of the video again and tell the story of each scene to your partner. You can use the keywords below.

e.g.
Keywords: director, roles, actors, staff
Model: Lauren is the director. She has many roles, including telling the actors and the staff what to do.

1. Keywords: Romain, director of photography, shot, lighting

2. Keywords: after, shoot, working, rest, edit

Discussion

Q: What kind of job in filmmaking are you most interested in? Why do you think so? What do you think about your partner's ideas?

Your ideas	Your partner's ideas

10

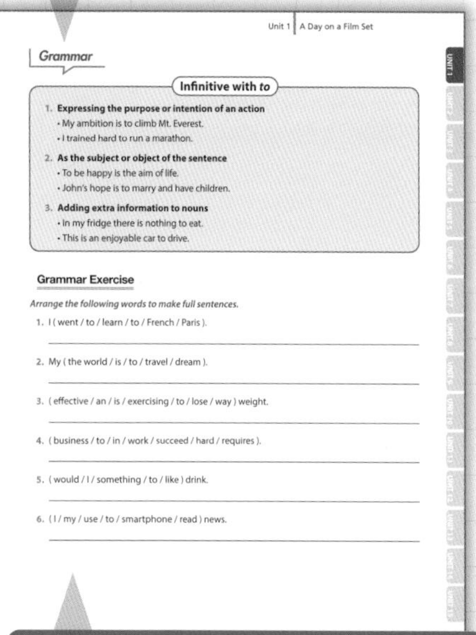

Unit 1 | A Day on a Film Set

Grammar

Infinitive with *to*

1. **Expressing the purpose or intention of an action**
   - My ambition is to climb Mt. Everest.
   - I trained hard to run a marathon.
2. **As the subject or object of the sentence**
   - To be happy is the aim of life.
   - John's hope is to marry and have children.
3. **Adding extra information to nouns**
   - In my fridge there is nothing to eat.
   - This is an enjoyable car to drive.

Grammar Exercise

Arrange the following words to make full sentences.

1. I (went / to / learn / to / French / Paris).
2. My (the world / is / to / travel / dream).
3. (effective / an / is / exercising / to / lose / way) weight.
4. (business / to / in / work / succeed / hard / requires).
5. (would / I / something / to / like) drink.
6. (I / my / use / to / smartphone / read) news.

Grammar Exercise

Enhances students' grammar ability through a word-order exercise.

Discussion

Presents a topic-related question to enhance students' critical thinking skills.

Vocabulary Check

Teaches useful vocabulary from the Reading.

Reading

Features an interesting article related to the topic of the video.

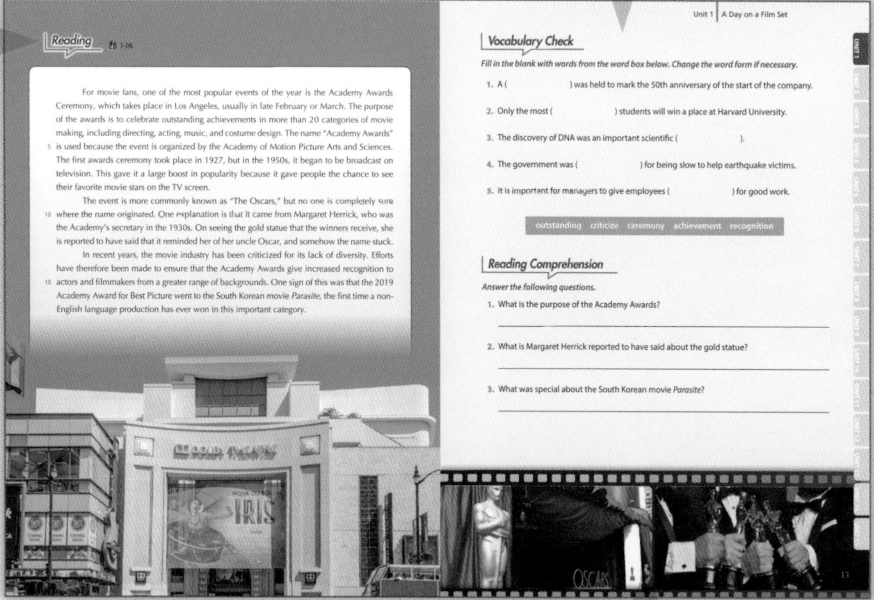

Reading 1-06

For movie fans, one of the most popular events of the year is the Academy Awards Ceremony, which takes place in Los Angeles, usually in late February or March. The purpose of the awards is to celebrate outstanding achievements in more than 20 categories of movie making, including directing, acting, music, and costume design. The name "Academy Awards" is used because the event is organized by the Academy of Motion Picture Arts and Sciences. The first awards ceremony took place in 1927, but in the 1950s, it began to be broadcast on television. This gave it a large boost in popularity because it gave people the chance to see their favorite movie stars on the TV screen.

The event is more commonly known as "The Oscars," but no one is completely sure where the name originated. One explanation is that it came from Margaret Herrick, who was the Academy's secretary in the 1930s. On seeing the gold statue that the winners receive, she is reported to have said that it reminded her of her uncle Oscar, and somehow the name stuck.

In recent years, the movie industry has been criticized for its lack of diversity. Efforts have therefore been made to ensure that the Academy Awards give increased recognition to actors and filmmakers from a greater range of backgrounds. One sign of this was that the 2019 Academy Award for Best Picture went to the South Korean movie *Parasite*, the first time a non-English language production has ever won in this important category.

Unit 1 | A Day on a Film Set

Vocabulary Check

Fill in the blank with words from the word box below. Change the word form if necessary.

1. A (　　　) was held to mark the 50th anniversary of the start of the company.
2. Only the most (　　　) students will win a place at Harvard University.
3. The discovery of DNA was an important scientific (　　　).
4. The government was (　　　) for being slow to help earthquake victims.
5. It is important for managers to give employees (　　　) for good work.

outstanding　criticize　ceremony　achievement　recognition

Reading Comprehension

Answer the following questions.

1. What is the purpose of the Academy Awards?
2. What is Margaret Herrick reported to have said about the gold statue?
3. What was special about the South Korean movie *Parasite*?

Reading Comprehension

Presents open-ended questions for students to check comprehension.

LEARNING OVERVIEW

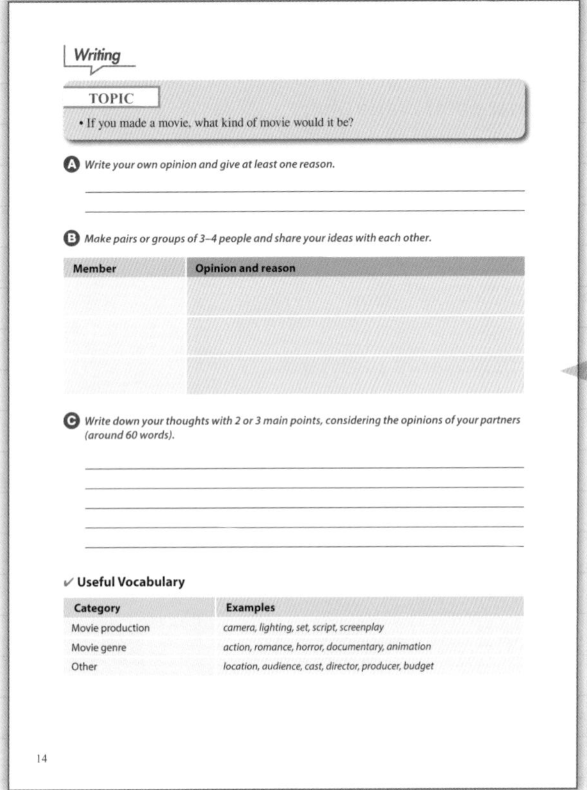

Writing

TOPIC

• If you made a movie, what kind of movie would it be?

A *Write your own opinion and give at least one reason.*

B *Make pairs or groups of 3–4 people and share your ideas with each other.*

Member	Opinion and reason

C *Write down your thoughts with 2 or 3 main points, considering the opinions of your partners (around 60 words).*

✓ **Useful Vocabulary**

Category	Examples
Movie production	*camera, lighting, set, script, screenplay*
Movie genre	*action, romance, horror, documentary, animation*
Other	*location, audience, cast, director, producer, budget*

14

Writing

Presents step-by-step exercises to aid output of students' ideas or opinions.

Useful Expressions for Discussions

Presents useful expressions for each discussion exercise.

Useful Expressions for Discussions

Starting a discussion

- ☐ Today, we are going to discuss …
- ☐ Today's topic is …
- ☐ Let's begin with …

Giving your opinion

- ☐ I think that … because …
- ☐ In my opinion, …
- ☐ I personally feel …
- ☐ As far as I am concerned, …
- ☐ I'm not sure, but perhaps …
- ☐ I strongly believe that …
- ☐ There's no doubt in my mind that …

Reacting

- ☐ I see.
- ☐ Really?
- ☐ That's interesting.
- ☐ Is that right?
- ☐ I didn't know that.
- ☐ Go on, please.

Asking for an opinion

- ☐ What do you think?
- ☐ What's your view?
- ☐ Do you agree?
- ☐ How about you?
- ☐ Could you tell me …?
- ☐ Could I have your opinion?

128

Agreeing

- ☐ I think so, too.
- ☐ I totally agree.
- ☐ I agree with you.
- ☐ That's a good point.
- ☐ I see what you mean.
- ☐ That is exactly what I think.
- ☐ Exactly.
- ☐ That makes sense.

Partially agreeing

- ☐ Yes, perhaps, but …
- ☐ That may be true, but …
- ☐ I suppose so. However, …
- ☐ You're right to a certain extent, but …
- ☐ Hmm …, it depends.

Disagreeing

- ☐ I don't think so.
- ☐ I disagree with you.
- ☐ I am afraid that is not quite true.
- ☐ I'm sorry, I really can't accept your idea.
- ☐ I take a different view.
- ☐ Actually, I think …

129

UNIT 1 A Day on a Film Set

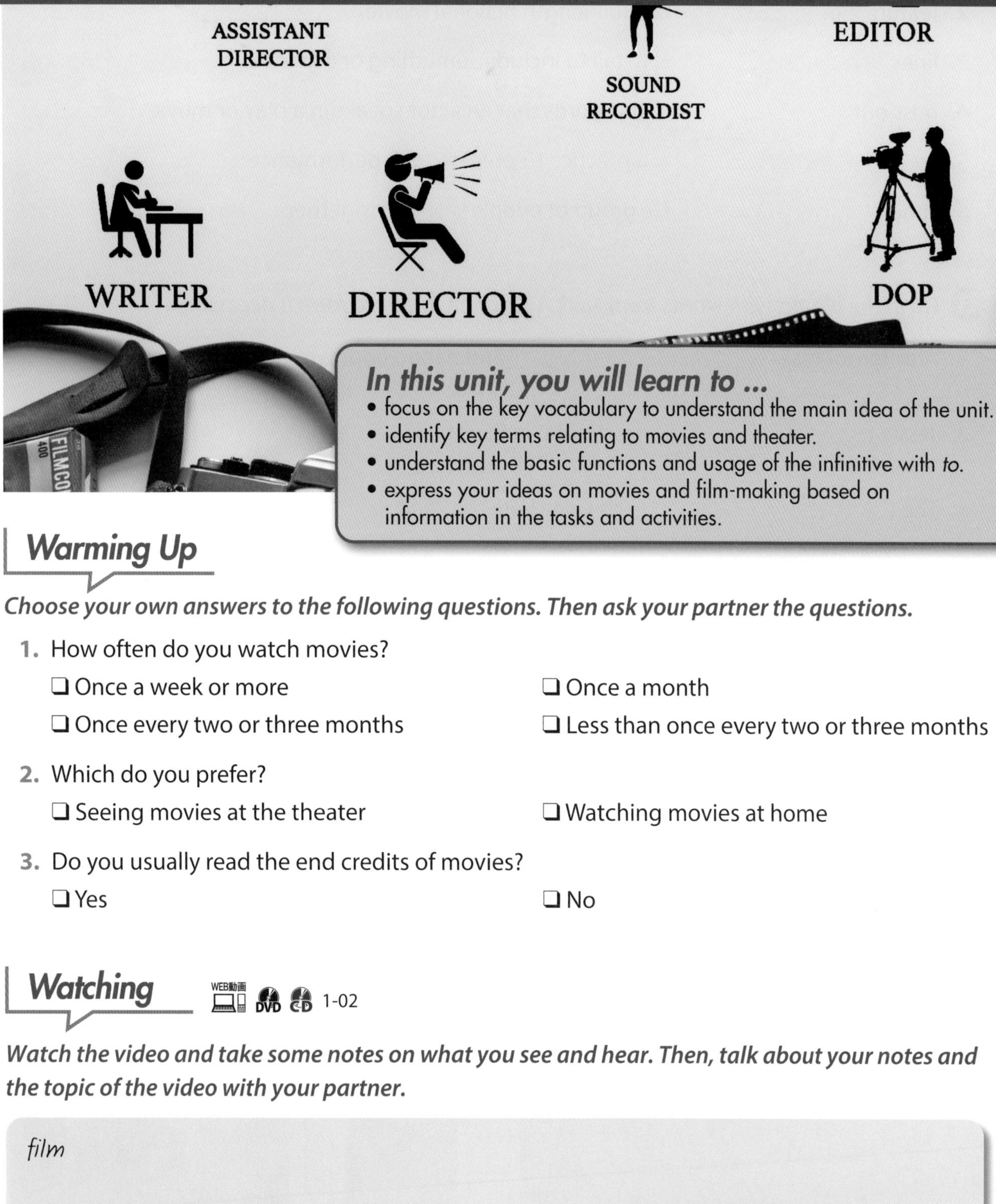

In this unit, you will learn to ...

- focus on the key vocabulary to understand the main idea of the unit.
- identify key terms relating to movies and theater.
- understand the basic functions and usage of the infinitive with *to*.
- express your ideas on movies and film-making based on information in the tasks and activities.

Warming Up

Choose your own answers to the following questions. Then ask your partner the questions.

1. How often do you watch movies?
   - ❏ Once a week or more
   - ❏ Once a month
   - ❏ Once every two or three months
   - ❏ Less than once every two or three months
2. Which do you prefer?
   - ❏ Seeing movies at the theater
   - ❏ Watching movies at home
3. Do you usually read the end credits of movies?
   - ❏ Yes
   - ❏ No

Watching

WEB動画 DVD CD 1-02

Watch the video and take some notes on what you see and hear. Then, talk about your notes and the topic of the video with your partner.

film

Vocabulary

1-03

A *Match the words and phrases below with the correct explanations (a – f).*

1. rehearsal	______	**a.** to take a video or photograph
2. feature film	______	**b.** a full-length fictional movie
3. lines	______	**c.** to fail to include something or someone
4. miss out	______	**d.** the words that an actor speaks in a play or movie
5. crew	______	**e.** a practice to prepare for a performance
6. shoot	______	**f.** a group of people working together

B *Fill in the blanks with words from Task A. Change the word form if necessary.*

1. Alex forgot his (   ) and had to improvise.

2. Jessie (   ) a film in Paris two years ago.

3. The (   ) is *Gone With the Wind.*

Listening Comprehension

WEB動画 DVD CD 1-02

A *Watch the video again and write T if the statement is true or F if it is false.*

1. Lauren, Sam, Romain, and Annais are part of a professional movie crew. ______

2. The most important document on a film set is the script. ______

3. Annais always works very hard to make the actors look good. ______

4. To make one movie, there are many people who are engaged in different jobs. ______

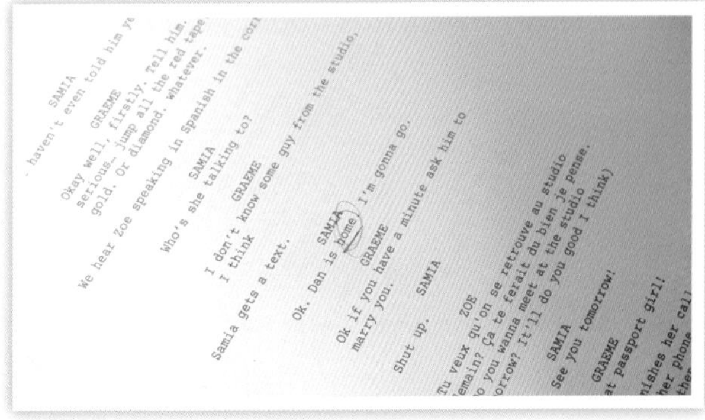

B *Match each job in film-making with its description by drawing lines.*

A. 
Director

B. 
DOP

C. 
Script supervisor

1. The person who oversees the continuity of shots.
2. The person in charge of managing the actors and crew members.
3. The person who oversees camera work.

Tips on Listening and Speaking

 1-04

Unreleased Stop Sound

When a consonant cluster has two stop sounds (i.e., p, t, k, b, d, g) in it, the first one is often unreleased.

1. She's the dire**c**tor and she's responsible for the whole film.
2. That's the a**c**tors, the camera team, the make-up artists and many others.
3. The most important document on a film set is the scri**p**t.

Dictation

 1-05

Listen to the sentences and fill in the blanks.

1. She tells the (   ) how to say their lines, and how to (   ) in each scene.
2. Sam checks that actors and other crew members follow the (   ) and don't miss out any lines or shots!
3. One of the ways he does that is to get the lighting (   ) right.

Retelling

Watch parts of the video again and tell the story of each scene to your partner. You can use the keywords below.

e.g.

Keywords

director, roles, actors, staff

Model

Lauren is the director. She has many roles, including telling the actors and the staff what to do.

1.

Keywords

Romain, director of photography, shot, lighting

2.

Keywords

after, shoot, working, rest, edit

Discussion

Q: *What kind of job in filmmaking are you most interested in? Why do you think so? What do you think about your partner's ideas?*

What do you think?

I think that … because …

Your ideas	Your partner's ideas

Grammar

Infinitive with *to*

1. **Expressing the purpose or intention of an action**
   - My ambition is to climb Mt. Everest.
   - I trained hard to run a marathon.
2. **As the subject or object of the sentence**
   - To be happy is the aim of life.
   - John's hope is to marry and have children.
3. **Adding extra information to nouns**
   - In my fridge there is nothing to eat.
   - This is an enjoyable car to drive.

Grammar Exercise

Arrange the following words to make full sentences.

1. I (went / to / learn / to / French / Paris).

   ____

2. My (the world / is / to / travel / dream).

   ____

3. (effective / an / is / exercising / to / lose / way) weight.

   ____

4. (business / to / in / work / succeed / hard / requires).

   ____

5. (would / I / something / to / like) drink.

   ____

6. (I / my / use / to / smartphone / read) news.

   ____

Reading

1-06

For movie fans, one of the most popular events of the year is the Academy Awards Ceremony, which takes place in Los Angeles, usually in late February or March. The purpose of the awards is to celebrate outstanding achievements in more than 20 categories of movie making, including directing, acting, music, and costume design. The name "Academy Awards" is used because the event is organized by the Academy of Motion Picture Arts and Sciences. The first awards ceremony took place in 1927, but in the 1950s, it began to be broadcast on television. This gave it a large boost in popularity because it gave people the chance to see their favorite movie stars on the TV screen.

The event is more commonly known as "The Oscars," but no one is completely sure where the name originated. One explanation is that it came from Margaret Herrick, who was the Academy's secretary in the 1930s. On seeing the gold statue that the winners receive, she is reported to have said that it reminded her of her uncle Oscar, and somehow the name stuck.

In recent years, the movie industry has been criticized for its lack of diversity. Efforts have therefore been made to ensure that the Academy Awards give increased recognition to actors and filmmakers from a greater range of backgrounds. One sign of this was that the 2019 Academy Award for Best Picture went to the South Korean movie *Parasite*, the first time a non-English language production has ever won in this important category.

Vocabulary Check

Fill in the blank with words from the word box below. Change the word form if necessary.

1. A ( ) was held to mark the 50th anniversary of the start of the company.
2. Only the most ( ) students will win a place at Harvard University.
3. The discovery of DNA was an important scientific ( ).
4. The government was ( ) for being slow to help earthquake victims.
5. It is important for managers to give employees ( ) for good work.

outstanding criticize ceremony achievement recognition

Reading Comprehension

Answer the following questions.

1. What is the purpose of the Academy Awards?

   ____

2. What is Margaret Herrick reported to have said about the gold statue?

   ____

3. What was special about the South Korean movie *Parasite*?

   ____

TOPIC

• If you made a movie, what kind of movie would it be?

A *Write your own opinion and give at least one reason.*

____

____

B *Make pairs or groups of 3–4 people and share your ideas with each other.*

Member	Opinion and reason

C *Write down your thoughts with 2 or 3 main points, considering the opinions of your partners (around 60 words).*

____

____

____

____

____

✔ Useful Vocabulary

Category	Examples
Movie production	*camera, lighting, set, script, screenplay*
Movie genre	*action, romance, horror, documentary, animation*
Other	*location, audience, cast, director, producer, budget*

UNIT 2 Jobray the Artist

In this unit, you will learn to ...

- focus on the key vocabulary to understand the main idea of the unit.
- identify key terms relating to art.
- understand the basic usage of post-modification.
- describe what you think are the most important things based on information in the tasks and activities.

Warming Up

Choose your own answers to the following questions. Then ask your partner the questions.

1. Which do you prefer?

❑ Realistic art ❑ Abstract art

2. What materials have you used to draw with?

❑ Colored pencils ❑ Crayons

❑ Watercolor paint ❑ Oil paint

❑ Acrylic paint ❑ Spray paint

3. Do you like art class?

❑ Yes ❑ No

Watching

WEB動画 DVD CD 1-07

Watch the video and take some notes on what you see and hear. Then, talk about your notes and the topic of the video with your partner.

art

Vocabulary

1-08

A *Match the words below with the correct explanations (a – f).*

1. capital ______
2. scribble ______
3. earn ______
4. community ______
5. mural ______
6. opportunity ______

a. to write or draw something quickly and carelessly
b. a large painting done on a wall
c. the city where the government of a country is located
d. an occasion that makes it possible to do or achieve something
e. to get money as payment for work
f. people who live in a particular area and who are considered as one group

B *Fill in the blanks with words from Task A. Change the word form if necessary.*

1. Chris is working two part-time jobs to (　　　　　　　　) money for school expenses.
2. This internship provides university students with a good (　　　　　　　　) to work at a global company.
3. I took part in a tour of six European (　　　　　　　　).

Listening Comprehension

WEB動画 DVD CD 1-07

A *Watch the video again and write T if the statement is true or F if it is false.*

1. Jobray first started doing art when he was around 10 years old. ______
2. His father and mother believed that he could be respected as an artist. ______
3. He likes painting in public spaces because it is important for him to communicate with others through his art. ______
4. He started teaching art to schoolchildren and teenagers because only young people like his art. ______

B ***Arrange the following events in the correct order.***

1. Jobray started teaching art to children.
2. Jobray got a job painting murals.
3. Jobray joined Breakdance Project Uganda.
4. Jobray traveled to Hamburg in Germany.

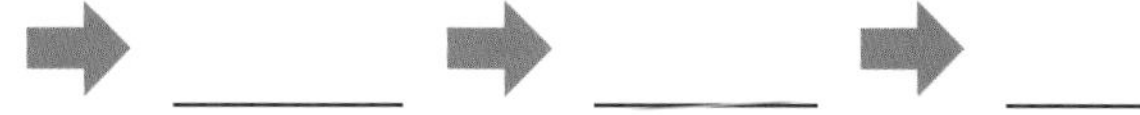

Tips on Listening and Speaking

 1-09

Dark /l/

"A dark /l/" sound occurs before a consonant or within a word.

1. He also had a bit of fun along the way!
2. They showed him it was possib**le** to have a career as an artist.
3. Last year, he traveled to Hamburg, in Germany, to work with some schoolchildren there.

Dictation

 1-10

Listen to the sentences and fill in the blanks.

1. And together, they used art in ( ) its forms to connect with ( ) in the community.
2. It ( ) him understand the ( ) around him.
3. He's ( ) young, but he's respected as an artist.

Retelling

WEB動画 DVD

Watch parts of the video again and tell the story of each scene to your partner. You can use the keywords below.

e.g.

Keywords

child, practiced, drawing, cartoon, comic books

Model

When he was a child, he practiced drawing every day and could draw cartoons like the ones in the comic books he saw.

1.

Keywords

artists, possibility, career, art, took part in

2.

Keywords

draw, walls, people, communicate

Discussion

Q: ***What is the most important thing you will need if you want to do something you like for a living? Why do you think so? What do you think about your partner's ideas?***

I strongly believe that …

That's a good point.

Your ideas	Your partner's ideas

Grammar

Post-modification

Post-modification refers to the process of adding extra information after a word or a phrase (post = after). This can be done in various ways.

1. **Using a relative clause**
   - This is the house that I lived in as a child.
   - The person who I was speaking to is my neighbor.
2. **Using a prepositional phrase**
   - The girl in the red dress is my sister.
   - The paintings in the gallery are very valuable.
3. **Using a participle**
   - I saw the student reading in the library.
   - The car parked outside is my father's.

Grammar Exercise

Arrange the following words to make full sentences.

1. I loved (movie / the / recommended / you / that).

   ____

2. (in / the band / are / the musicians) talented.

   ____

3. (I / the children / with / watched / playing / a ball).

   ____

4. (in / chair / the / is / placed) the corner.

   ____

5. The city (New York / is / grew up / I / where).

   ____

6. (on / the book / top / the / down / shelf / fell).

   ____

Reading

1-11

To see art, you no longer have to visit a gallery or a museum. Beautiful, striking images can now be seen on the streets of major cities around the world, often in the form of murals. When colorful graffiti began appearing on the sides of buildings and subway trains in New York in the 1960s, city authorities considered this type of public art as ugly and destructive. But as time went on, people came to appreciate the skill and vision of the best graffiti artists, and "street art" began to be appreciated and viewed much more positively.

Many communities now understand that street art such as murals can bring enormous benefits. Murals brighten up dull city streets, bringing color and beauty into people's lives. They can also attract visitors to neighborhoods, giving a boost to local businesses and helping bring areas back to life. Not only that, they can also provide a meaningful way for talented young artists from those neighborhoods to exhibit their skills.

Beautify Earth is an organization that brings together mural artists to work on various projects across the United States. For example, it has helped to turn Santa Monica, close to Los Angeles, into one of the street art capitals of the world. The area around the center now has more than 120 murals, which attract constant streams of visitors.

Vocabulary Check

Fill in the blank with words from the word box below. Change the word form if necessary.

1. Recently, the ( ) has been showing works by young local artists.
2. My grandfather taught me how to ( ) classical music.
3. Regular exercise has many ( ) for your health.
4. The school concert gave many students the chance to ( ) their talents.
5. People like drinking coffee because it gives them a ( ) in energy.

benefit	appreciate	boost	gallery	exhibit

Reading Comprehension

Answer the following questions.

1. How did city authorities consider graffiti in the 1960s?

____

2. What are some of the positive effects of murals?

____

3. What does the organization Beautify Earth want to do?

____

TOPIC

- Why do you think art education is valuable?

A *Write your own opinion and give at least one reason.*

____

____

B *Make pairs or groups of 3–4 people and share your ideas with each other.*

Member	Opinion and reason

C *Write down your thoughts with 2 or 3 main points, considering the opinions of your partners (around 60 words).*

____

____

____

____

____

✔ Useful Vocabulary

Category	Examples
Education	*graduate, course, bachelor's/master's degree*
Art	*painting, sculpture, gallery*
Other	*culture, humanities, expertise*

UNIT 3

Horseback Library

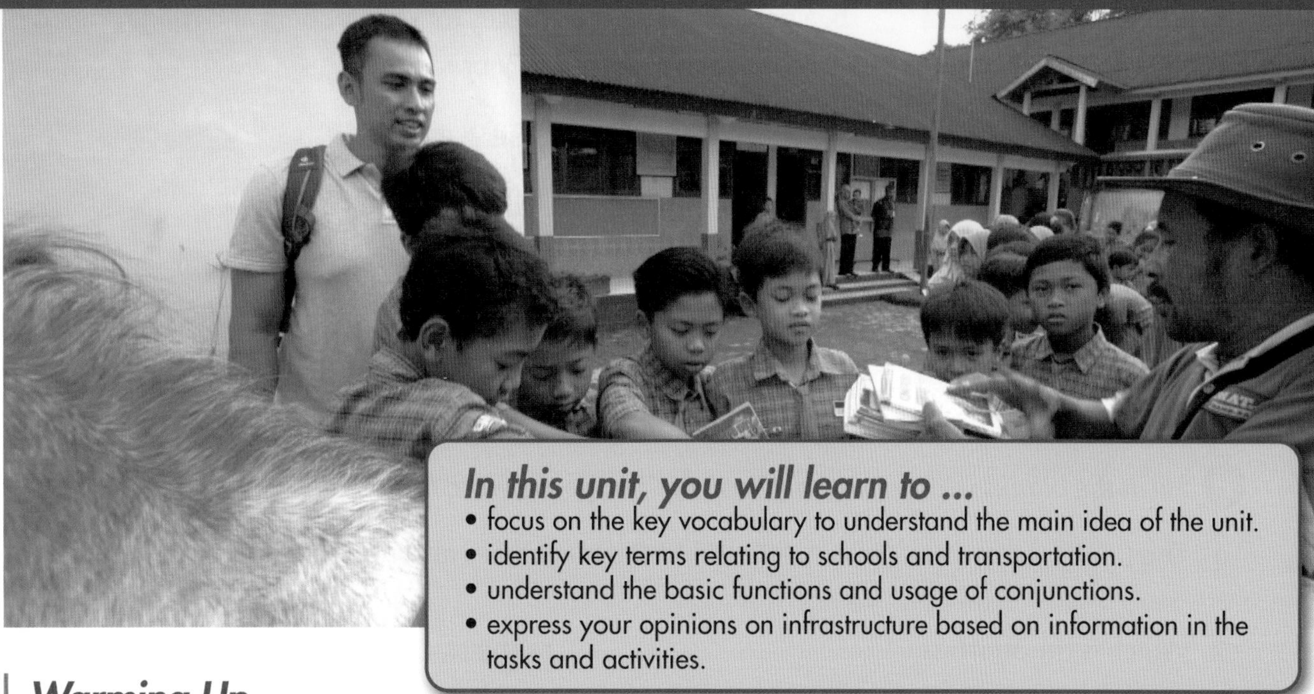

In this unit, you will learn to ...

- focus on the key vocabulary to understand the main idea of the unit.
- identify key terms relating to schools and transportation.
- understand the basic functions and usage of conjunctions.
- express your opinions on infrastructure based on information in the tasks and activities.

Warming Up

Choose your own answers to the following questions. Then ask your partner the questions.

1. When you were in elementary school, how often did you go to the library?
   - ❑ Often
   - ❑ Sometimes
   - ❑ Rarely
   - ❑ Other
2. Which do you prefer to read?
   - ❑ Paper books
   - ❑ E-books
3. What genre do you like to read?
   - ❑ Novels
   - ❑ Essays
   - ❑ Comics
   - ❑ Other (   )

Watching

WEB動画 DVD CD 1-12

Watch the video and take some notes on what you see and hear. Then, talk about your notes and the topic of the video with your partner.

traveler

Vocabulary

CD 1-13

A *Match the words below with the correct explanations (a – f).*

1. journalist ______
2. island ______
3. librarian ______
4. steep ______
5. climb ______
6. route ______

a. rising or falling at a high angle
b. a person who writes pieces for newspapers and magazines, or broadcasts reports on TV or radio
c. a person who is in charge of a library
d. a piece of land surrounded by water
e. to go upward on something
f. a particular way to travel from one place to another

B *Fill in the blanks with words from Task A. Change the word form if necessary.*

1. The (   ) classified the magazines according to category and author.
2. Which is the shortest (   ) to the station?
3. Some small (   ) are sinking because the ice in Antarctica is melting and sea levels are rising.

Listening Comprehension

WEB動画 DVD CD 1-12

A *Watch the video again and write T if the statement is true or F if it is false.*

1. Khairudin is collaborating with a librarian. ______
2. Children in the local primary school are happy to see the horseback library because they can ride the horses. ______
3. To walk up the mountain off-road is difficult for Khairudin and Ridwan, but not for the horses. ______
4. Some children in Indonesia cannot go to school. ______

B *What types of route did they take? Choose and circle the correct one for each step.*

Ridwan's house

Hillside → Bayside

Primary school

Lasmi's house

Tips on Listening and Speaking

 1-14

Dropping /h/ (Weak Form)

When the pronoun (i.e., *he, his, him, her*) or auxiliary verbs (i.e., *have, has, had*) are not highlighted or emphasized in a sentence, /h/ is often unpronounced.

1. The normal route that **he** normally takes, the road is under repair, so we can't use that road, so we **have** to trek!
2. Ridwan's library is very important to **her**.

Dictation

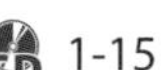 1-15

Listen to the sentences and fill in the blanks.

1. He (　　　　　) (　　　　　) (　　　　　) to carry books to schools and children in the local community.
2. The team (　　　　　) (　　　　　) walk up the mountain off-road.
3. Today, they've also brought some coloring books and pens (　　　　　) (　　　　　).

Retelling

WEB動画 DVD

Watch parts of the video again and tell the story of each scene to your partner. You can use the keywords below.

e.g.

Keywords

Ridwan, carry, climb, roads

Model

Ridwan uses horses to carry books because they can climb a mountain with no roads.

1.

Keywords

Java, volcanoes, mountains, jungles, hard

2.

Keywords

Ridwan's library, Lasmi, books, school

Discussion

Q: ***If you were Ridwan, how often would you visit the school and Lasmi's house? Why do you think so? What do you think about your partner's ideas?***

I personally feel …

I totally agree.

Your ideas	Your partner's ideas

Grammar

Conjunctions

Conjunctions are used to join words, phrases, and clauses.

1. **Coordinating Conjunctions**

They join things that are equally important. For example: *and, or, nor, but, yet, so.*

- I got up and I made breakfast.
- I wanted to go out, but I was too tired.

2. **Subordinating Conjunctions**

These connect main clauses and subordinate clauses. For example: *when, after, before, because, although, since, unless,* etc.

- Jack woke up when he heard his alarm.
- I drink coffee because it gives me energy.

3. **Correlative Conjunctions**

These always come in pairs. For example: *either...or, neither...nor, both...and, not only...but also.*

- I either read a book or watch TV in the evenings.
- Jim likes both cats and dogs.

Grammar Exercise

Arrange the following words to make full sentences.

1. (we / hamburgers / or / can / have / either) pizza.

____

2. (the audience / when / ended / the performance / applauded).

____

3. (the book / boring / was / stopped / I / reading / so).

____

4. (enjoy / I / tried / I / didn't / it / jogging / but).

____

5. (here / have / I / lived / I / was / since) born.

____

6. (my / both / mother / doctors / are / father and / my).

____

Reading

1-16

Britain's famous red public telephone boxes were once a common sight all over the country. But since the widespread adoption of mobile phones, they are rapidly disappearing. Many British people felt sad to lose them and wondered how they could save them.

In 2009, BT (Britain's main telephone company) launched a program called "Adopt a Kiosk." This project allows local communities to "adopt" a telephone box for a very low rent and use it for a different purpose. BT simply removes the phones and leaves the structures in place. Since 2009, more than 1,500 kiosks have been changed in this way.

One of the most popular new uses is as a public library. The way it works is like this. If people have books that they no longer want, they can take them to the telephone box library and leave them on the shelves. People are then free to borrow a book on condition that they replace it with one of their own. This ensures that the stock of books of this "library" stays at the same level.

This system has numerous good points. For one thing, it preserves familiar structures that remind local people of their history. For another, it is a great help to people who love to read but who may not have enough money to buy new books. What is more, it gives people the chance to help others by contributing something to the local community.

Vocabulary Check

Fill in the blank with words from the word box below. Change the word form if necessary.

1. Because of the warm weather, the snow (   ) very quickly.
2. The workers (   ) the damaged window and fitted a new one.
3. I need to (   ) money from the bank to buy an apartment.
4. People from (   ) countries now enjoy skiing in Hokkaido.
5. Many people (   ) their time to help clean up the local beaches.

remove	numerous	disappear	contribute	borrow

Reading Comprehension

Answer the following questions.

1. What structures are rapidly disappearing in Britain?

   ____

2. What is one condition for borrowing a book from a telephone box library?

   ____

3. What kind of people can telephone box libraries help?

   ____

TOPIC

• Which do you think is more important for city development, transportation infrastructure or internet infrastructure?

A *Write your own opinion and give at least one reason.*

____

____

B *Make pairs or groups of 3–4 people and share your ideas with each other.*

Member	Opinion and reason

C *Write down your thoughts with 2 or 3 main points, considering the opinions of your partners (around 60 words).*

____

____

____

____

____

✔ Useful Vocabulary

Category	Examples
Transportation	*bus/train/rail network, commuting, travel time, connections*
Internet	*cable, optical fiber, video conferencing, broadband access*
Other	*remote working, time-saving, efficient*

UNIT 4

Arctic Football

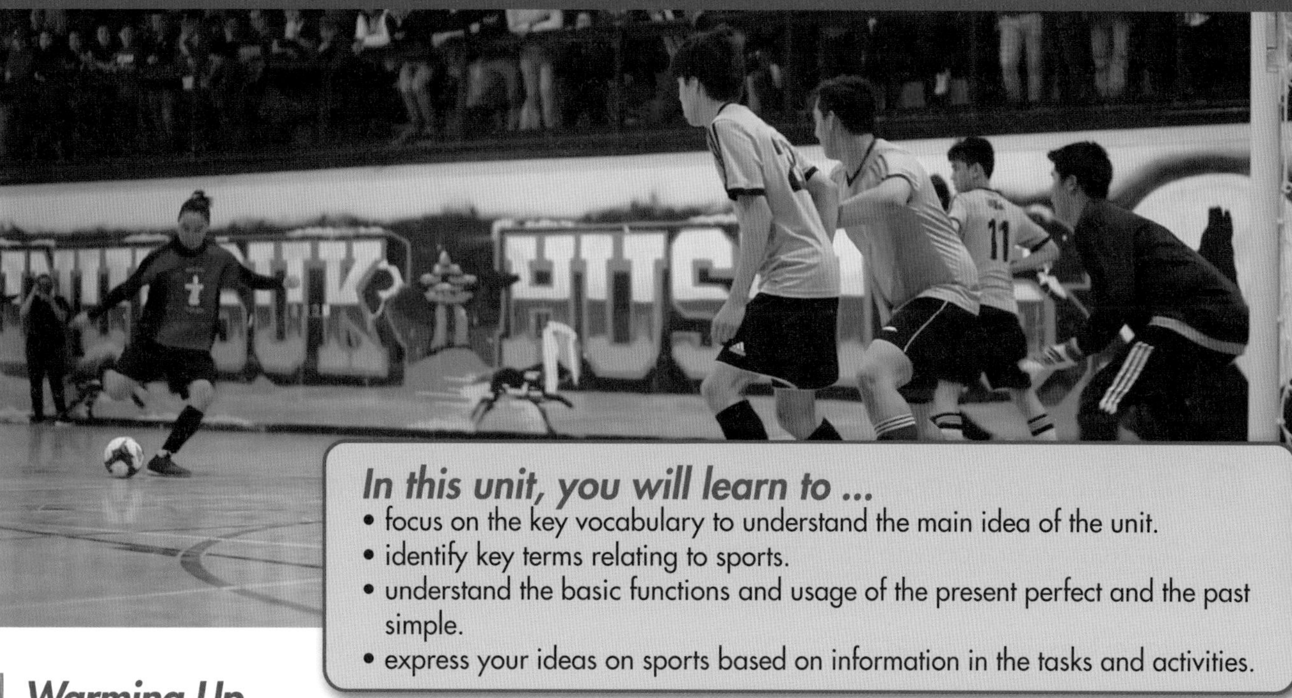

In this unit, you will learn to ...

- focus on the key vocabulary to understand the main idea of the unit.
- identify key terms relating to sports.
- understand the basic functions and usage of the present perfect and the past simple.
- express your ideas on sports based on information in the tasks and activities.

Warming Up

Choose your own answers to the following questions. Then ask your partner the questions.

1. What sports do you like?
   - ❑ Soccer
   - ❑ Swimming
   - ❑ Judo
   - ❑ Other ( )
2. Which do you prefer?
   - ❑ Playing sports
   - ❑ Watching sports
3. How often do you play sports?
   - ❑ Once a week or more
   - ❑ Once a month
   - ❑ Once every two or three months
   - ❑ Less than once every two or three months

Watching

WEB動画 DVD CD 1-17

Watch the video and take some notes on what you see and hear. Then, talk about your notes and the topic of the video with your partner.

soccer

Vocabulary 1-18

A *Match the words below with the correct explanations (a – f).*

1. temperature ______
2. captain ______
3. team ______
4. goal ______
5. tournament ______
6. rule ______

a. a sports competition with many games to determine the champion
b. the leader of a team
c. a point that is scored in a game
d. a statement of what people can or cannot do in a game
e. the measurement of how hot or cold something is
f. a group of people who play a sport or game against other groups

B *Fill in the blanks with words from Task A. Change the word form if necessary.*

1. Our team won a prize in the national (   ).
2. Lionel Messi has scored 13 (   ) in 26 matches across five World Cups.
3. The average (   ) in Japan has been going up every year.

Listening Comprehension WEB動画 DVD CD 1-17

A *Watch the video again and write T if the statement is true or F if it is false.*

1. Soccer is popular all over the Arctic North of Canada. ______
2. In Iqaluit, playing sports is good for not only physical but also mental health. ______
3. Soccer is a new sport in Iqaluit. ______
4. The teams are playing the traditional game at the soccer tournament in Iqaluit. ______

B *What are the similarities and differences between soccer and Aqijuq? Circle the correct answers below.*

e.g.) Players use a ball.	Only soccer	Both	Only Aqijuq
1. Players play on the pitch.	Only soccer	Both	Only Aqijuq
2. There are no goalposts.	Only soccer	Both	Only Aqijuq
3. Players try to score goals.	Only soccer	Both	Only Aqijuq
4. Players run as far as they can.	Only soccer	Both	Only Aqijuq
5. It is a team game.	Only soccer	Both	Only Aqijuq

Tips on Listening and Speaking

 1-19

Linking /r/-Colored Vowel + Vowel

When a vowel comes after an /r/-colored vowel, /ɚ/ is pronounced like /ə/ + /r/.

1. The team spirit of socce**r** is very important for many people.
2. The**re** is an Inuit legend about the aurora borealis or northern lights.

Dictation

 1-20

Listen to the sentences and fill in the blanks.

1. Soccer has been part of our culture (　　　　) (　　　　) very long time.
2. There's no pitch and (　　　　) (　　　　) no lines or goalposts.
3. It's the highlight of the soccer (　　　　) (　　　　) the North.

Retelling

WEB動画 DVD

Watch parts of the video again and tell the story of each scene to your partner. You can use the keywords below.

e.g.

Keywords

Iqaluit, temperature, minus 40 degrees Celsius, live

Model

To live in Iqaluit can be difficult because the temperature can reach minus 40 degrees Celsius.

1.

Keywords

traditional Inuit football, different, for example, no lines or goalposts, run

2.

Keywords

eight, boys, girls, tournament, Canada

Discussion

Q: *Which team sport is the best for people living in hot areas? Why do you think so? What do you think about your partner's ideas?*

I'm not sure, but perhaps …

I see what you mean.

Your ideas	Your partner's ideas

Grammar

Present Perfect Simple vs Past Simple

We use the present perfect simple tense (*have/has + past participle*) to describe unfinished actions that began in the past and continue up to the present time. We use the past simple tense to describe actions or events that began and ended at a particular time in the past.

1. **With *for***

If we want to talk about the length/duration of the action, we use *for.*

- Tom lives in Barcelona. He has lived there for 10 years.
- John and Maria are married. They have been married for three months.

2. **With *since***

If we want to talk about the starting point of the action, we use *since.*

- Julie studies math. She has studied it since she was five years old.
- Paul lives in London. He has lived there since he was born.

3. **Past Simple**

Use the past simple tense to describe actions and events that are finished.

- He got married last year.
- He passed his driving test when he was 18.

Grammar Exercise

Arrange the following words to make full sentences.

1. (London / two / I've / in / lived / for) years.

____

2. Lauren (the piano / has / years / played / ten / for).

____

3. (Joe / in / Harvard University / studied / the / at) 1990s.

____

4. I've (elementary school / known / in the same class / since / Sophia / were / we / at).

____

5. (aikido / studied / for / Tom / several) years.

____

6. My father (was / he / cheese / a young / has / since / disliked / child).

____

Reading

1-21

Aqijuq is not the only unusual sport in the world. There are many more. For example, competitive eating may be familiar to people in Japan because one of the most successful competitors is Japanese. Takeru Kobayashi, who has won the world championship six times, has become known as "the Godfather of competitive eating." A popular sport in Finland is wife carrying. As the name suggests, men compete to see who can carry their wives the fastest over a certain distance. And there are sports in which humans do not even need to be involved, including surfing competitions for dogs, especially in the USA.

One of the most unusual sports combines two skills that appear to be the exact opposite of each other, one entirely mental and the other extremely physical. This unlikely activity is chess boxing. It takes place in a normal boxing ring. After the two opponents have completed a round of boxing, a chess board is set up in the ring, and they play a round of time-controlled speed chess. The winner is decided either by victory in boxing (knockout or points) or by victory in chess (checkmate or time penalties).

The first chess boxing championship was held in Berlin in 2003. The sport has since grown in popularity, and today tournaments are held around the world. The countries where it is most popular include the UK, France, Russia, and India.

Vocabulary Check

Fill in the blank with words from the word box below. Change the word form if necessary.

1. I don't understand rugby because I'm not ( ) with all the rules.
2. Some ( ) in the marathon were unable to complete the race.
3. The movie ( ) powerful acting and a moving story.
4. We will face a strong ( ) in the soccer game on Saturday.
5. The coach hopes that his new training methods will result in ( ).

familiar	opponent	victory	combine	competitor

Reading Comprehension

Answer the following questions.

1. How did Takeru Kobayashi earn his nickname?

____

2. Why do chess and boxing seem to be an unlikely combination of activities?

____

3. How is the winner decided in chess boxing?

____

TOPIC

- Are esports really sports?

A *Write your own opinion and give at least one reason.*

____

____

B *Make pairs or groups of 3–4 people and share your ideas with each other.*

Member	Opinion and reason

C *Write down your thoughts with 2 or 3 main points, considering the opinions of your partners (around 60 words).*

____

____

____

____

____

✔ Useful Vocabulary

Category	Examples
Esports	*console, streamers, gamers, competition, tournament*
Ability	*expert, mental agility, fast reflexes, coordination, concentration*
Other	*athleticism, teamwork, cooperation, determination, endurance*

UNIT 5

Transformer Boy

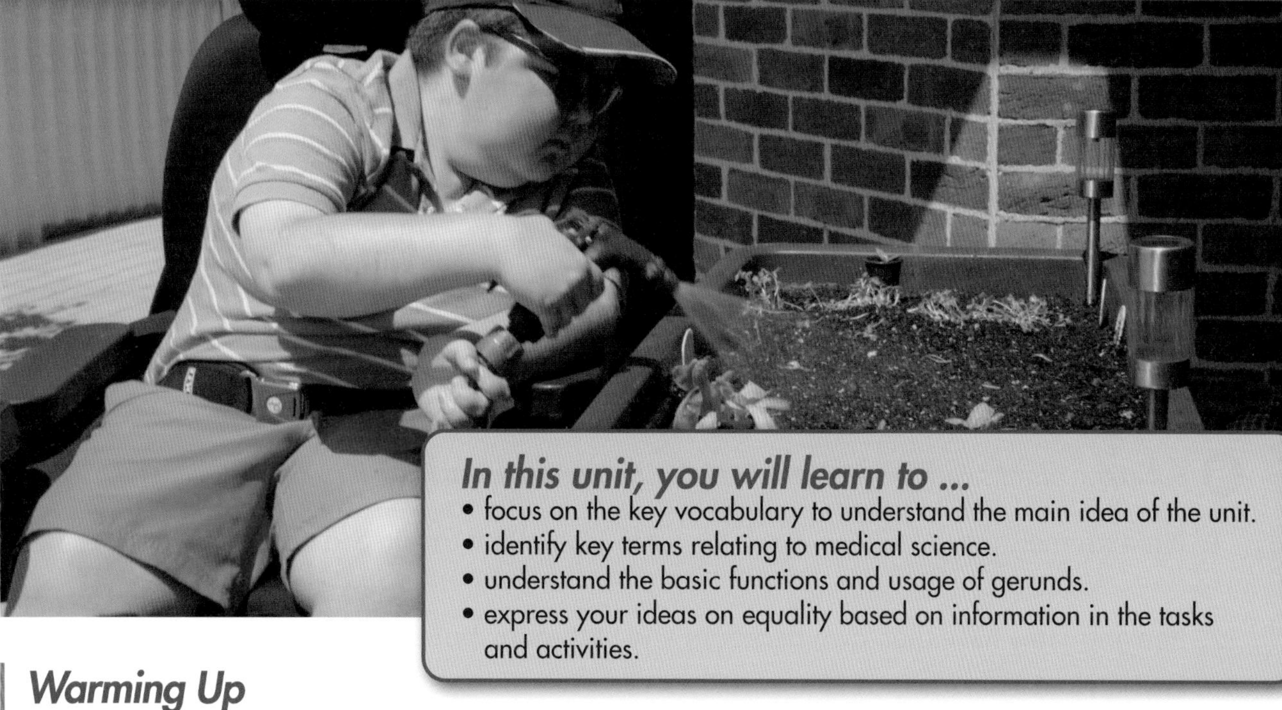

In this unit, you will learn to ...

- focus on the key vocabulary to understand the main idea of the unit.
- identify key terms relating to medical science.
- understand the basic functions and usage of gerunds.
- express your ideas on equality based on information in the tasks and activities.

Warming Up

Choose your own answers to the following questions. Then ask your partner the questions.

1. What are you good at?
   - ❑ Swimming fast
   - ❑ Singing
   - ❑ Cooking
   - ❑ Other (   )
2. Do you have a pet? If your answer is "No," what animal do you want to have?
   - ❑ Dog
   - ❑ Bird
   - ❑ Turtle
   - ❑ Other (   )
3. What do you usually do when you spend time with your friends?
   - ❑ Have lunch/dinner
   - ❑ Play sports
   - ❑ Go shopping
   - ❑ Other (   )

Watching

WEB動画 DVD CD 1-22

Watch the video and take some notes on what you see and hear. Then, talk about your notes and the topic of the video with your partner.

wheelchair

Vocabulary

1-23

A *Match the words and phrases below with the correct explanations (a – f).*

1. rare ______
2. function ______
3. in charge ______
4. provide ______
5. therapy ______
6. share ______

a. to have, use, or experience something with others
b. to give something to someone or make it available for them to use
c. the natural purpose of a person or thing
d. treatment of an injury or illness
e. not frequent
f. responsible for something or someone

B *Fill in the blanks with words from Task A. Change the word form if necessary.*

1. It is extremely ( ) in Japan for it to rain a lot in winter.
2. Ren and Jamy have their own bedroom and bathroom, but ( ) a kitchen and a garage.
3. We ( ) the affected people with tents and meals.

Listening Comprehension

WEB動画 DVD CD 1-22

A *Watch the video again and write T if the statement is true or F if it is false.*

1. Scott cannot walk because he was badly injured in an accident. ______
2. Scott can always be strong because he can do things with his wheelchair. ______
3. Scott's chickens lay eggs every day. ______
4. Scott's best friends at school call him chef when they cook. ______

B *Choose the things that Scott enjoys in the video.*

☐	running in the garden	☐	watering the plants
☐	feeding his pets	☐	swimming in the pool
☐	cooking	☐	playing video games

Tips on Listening and Speaking

 1-24

Double Consonants

Double consonants after a short vowel are pronounced as one consonant. This means that a vowel before double consonants is pronounced as a short vowel.

1. But the **rabbit** is the one who's really in charge.
2. The boys have a great time together because they enjoy the same activities, like cooking and **swimming**.

Dictation

 1-25

Listen to the sentences and fill in the blanks.

1. That's where Scott's (   ) come in.
2. I feed them corn cobs, which they love to peck at, and they come (   ) from nowhere and just basically (   ) it.
3. My life is (   ), but I do want to be treated like anyone else.

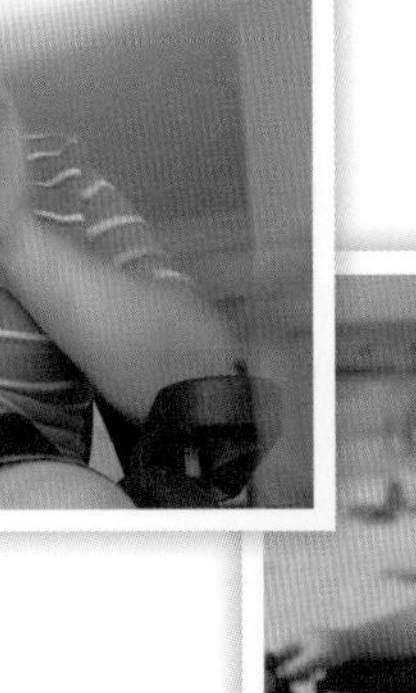

Retelling

WEB動画 DVD

Watch parts of the video again and tell the story of each scene to your partner. You can use the keywords below.

e.g.

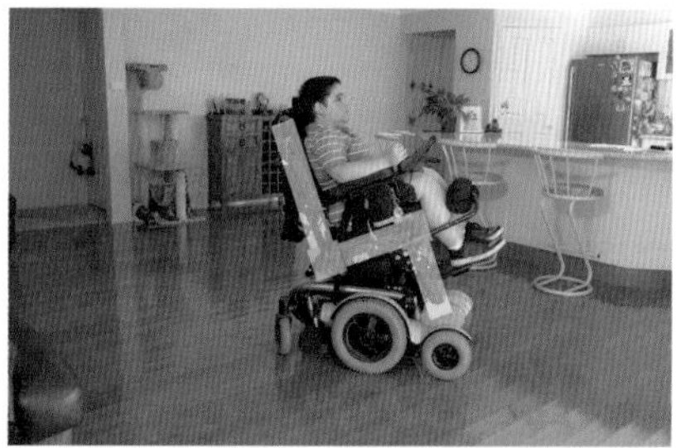

Keywords

Scott's disease, prevent, walk, by himself, can, electric wheelchair

Model

Scott's disease prevents him from walking by himself, but he can stand up by using his electric wheelchair.

1.

Keywords

Scott and his friends, fun time, doing, together

2.

Keywords

Scott, live, two friends, the same disease

Discussion

Q: ***If you were Scott's friend, what would you do with him on his birthday? Why do you think so? What do you think about your partner's ideas?***

What I'm trying to say is …

That is exactly what I think.

Your ideas	Your partner's ideas

Grammar

Gerunds

Gerunds are nouns formed from verbs by adding *-ing* to the base form (dropping the final *e* if necessary), e.g., *go + ing → going, mak(e) + ing → making.*

1. **Gerunds as Nouns**
   Gerunds can function as the subject or object of a sentence:
   - Swimming is my favorite sport.
   - I enjoy cooking.
2. **Gerunds in Phrasal Verbs**
   For example: *put off, call off, look forward to, get over.*
   - I put off going to the dentist because I was busy.
   - Jack is looking forward to going on vacation.
3. **Gerunds after Adjective-Preposition combinations**
   For example: *tired of, bored with, afraid of, worried about, interested in.*
   - I'm interested in discovering more about other cultures.
   - Kayla is worried about living on her own.

Grammar Exercise

Arrange the words to make full sentences.

1. (won't / complaining / problems / solve / about) them.

   ____

2. (weekends / I'm / not / on / working / to / accustomed).

   ____

3. (looking / Sue / job / is / changing / into / her).

   ____

4. (is / leaving / Mike / about / on / vacation / happy).

   ____

5. (car / my / be / expensive / repairing / will / quite).

   ____

6. (running / I / took over / the company / from / father / my).

   ____

Reading

1-26

Rare diseases are a more widespread problem than most people imagine. It is estimated that there are between 7,000 and 10,000 rare illnesses, which affect 25-30 million people in the United States alone. For people suffering from rare diseases, getting suitable medical support is often difficult. Treatment is often expensive and hard to find. What is more, because some of the diseases affect only a small number of people, there is not much money for research into developing new drugs and other treatments.

It is estimated that effective treatments are available for only five percent of rare diseases. Therefore, one of the most effective ways to help people with such diseases is to offer psychological support. People with rare diseases can often feel very isolated and cut off from society. This can lead to problems with mental health in addition to their severe physical problems. This is why support groups are so important. Such groups have several benefits. They allow people to develop social ties, share common experiences, and exchange advice on treatment options.

It is also important to consider family members who are caring for people with rare diseases. Experienced volunteer caregivers should be encouraged to look after patients temporarily so that the family members can take a break and refresh themselves.

Vocabulary Check

Fill in the blank with words from the word box below. Change the word form if necessary.

1. I ( ) that the construction work will take about three weeks.

2. It took several years to develop an effective ( ) for the illness.

3. Mary felt very ( ) when she went abroad to study.

4. One of the most important things for happiness is to have strong ( ) with others.

5. I learned a lot from the more ( ) players on my soccer team.

treatment isolated tie estimate experienced

Reading Comprehension

Answer the following questions.

1. What is true of treatment for rare diseases?

____

2. Why do people with rare diseases have problems with their mental health?

____

3. How can we help family members of patients with rare diseases?

____

Writing

TOPIC

- If you designed a public building that is accessible to everyone, which features would you include?

A *Write your own opinion and give at least one reason.*

____

____

B *Make pairs or groups of 3–4 people and share your ideas with each other.*

Member	Opinion and reason

C *Write down your thoughts with 2 or 3 main points, considering the opinions of your partners (around 60 words).*

____

____

____

____

____

✔ Useful Vocabulary

Category	Examples
Buildings	*station, city office, sports stadium, public facility*
People	*wheelchair user, disability, physically challenged, mobility problems*
Other	*barrier-free, universal design, easy access, ramp*

UNIT 6 Volunteer Hairdresser

In this unit, you will learn to ...
- focus on the key vocabulary to understand the main idea of the unit.
- identify key terms relating to volunteer activities.
- understand the basic usage of SVOC sentences.
- express your ideas on volunteer activities based on information in the tasks and activities.

Warming Up

Choose your own answers to the following questions. Then ask your partner the questions.

1. What kind of volunteer activity can you join in your community?
   - ❑ Environmental protection　　❑ Animal protection
   - ❑ Child welfare　　❑ Other (　　　　　　　　)
2. Which activity are you most interested in now?
   - ❑ Environmental protection　　❑ Animal protection
   - ❑ Child welfare　　❑ Other (　　　　　　　　)
3. Have you ever participated in volunteer work?
   - ❑ Yes　　❑ No

Watching

WEB動画 DVD CD 1-27

Watch the video and take some notes on what you see and hear. Then, talk about your notes and the topic of the video with your partner.

hairdresser

Vocabulary

CD 1-28

A *Match the words and phrases below with the correct explanations (a – f).*

1. difference ______
2. volunteer ______
3. free ______
4. project ______
5. get involved ______
6. look after ______

a. a planned piece of work to achieve a particular purpose
b. the way in which two or more people or things are not the same
c. to take care of or to be responsible for someone or something
d. costing nothing
e. to offer to do something of one's own free will without payment
f. to become part of something

B *Fill in the blanks with words from Task A. Change the word form if necessary.*

1. Brook is a math teacher and sometimes (   ) as a translator for Chinese parents.

2. Chris and Tracy (   ) their grandchildren every weekend.

3. Eight employees in this company will (   ) in international business training in Amsterdam.

Listening Comprehension

WEB動画 DVD CD 1-27

A *Watch the video again and write T if the statement is true or F if it is false.*

1. Josh gives inexpensive haircuts to the homeless. ______
2. Josh started Do Something for Nothing in 2005. ______
3. Jade is a doctor who looks after Josh's dog. ______
4. Giving time and skills to the community makes Josh happy. ______

B ***What is a big part of Josh and Jade's work in East London? Complete the sentence with appropriate phrases (A-F) from the box below.***

A big part of Josh and Jade's work is (   ) in the community and (   ).

A. helping homeless people	**D.** speaking to people
B. learning about their lives	**E.** providing medicines
C. giving haircuts	**F.** solving all of people's problems

Tips on Listening and Speaking

 1-29

Consonant Cluster of /t, d/ + /r/

The sequence /t/ + /d/ and /d/ + /r/ are similar to /ʧ/ and /ʤ/.

1. Josh Coombes is a hair**dr**esser who wants to make a small difference to people's lives.
2. I'm a hair**dr**esser and recently I've been going out on the s**tr**eet to cut hair for those who are homeless.

Dictation

 1-30

Listen to the sentences and fill in the blanks.

1. This was when I started going (   ) (   ) (   ) (   ) with my scissors, to cut hair for people who need it.

2. (   ) (   ) (   ) (   ) people who like a photo, or a thousand people who see a video, you don't know which one of those is gonna go "actually, I feel like this is for me too."

3. Just stop and just see how someone's doing, (   ) (   ) (   ) some community, some friendship. I think that's really, really important, isn't it, mate?

Retelling

WEB動画 DVD

Watch parts of the video again and tell the story of each scene to your partner. You can use the keywords below.

e.g.

Keywords

Josh, started, makes, people in the community, as well as himself, happy

Model

Josh started a project to show people that helping others makes people in the community happy as well as making himself happy.

1.

Keywords

Josh, photos, other people, his community

2.

Keywords

even if, talking, can, make people

Discussion

Q: What is one problem in your community, and what can you do to solve this problem as a university student? Why do you think so? What do you think about your partner's ideas?

Could you tell us a bit more about that?

For example, …

Your ideas	Your partner's ideas

Grammar

SVOC Sentences

SVOC refers to the different components of a sentence: S = subject; V = verb; O = object; C = complement. This is one of the most common sentence patterns in English. "Complement" refers to an adjective or a noun that provides more information about the object of the sentence. A simple example of this is the sentence *I call my dog Barney*, where *I* is the subject, *call* is the verb, *my dog* is the object, and *Barney* is the complement.

1. **Adjective as Complement**
   - The noise drove me crazy.
   - We painted the wall blue.
2. **Noun/Noun Phrase as Complement**
   - He declared the meeting a great success.
   - I find him a helpful colleague.
3. **Complement with Verbs of Thought/Feeling/Opinion**
   When using complements with verbs such as *think, consider, believe, know, and suppose,* the verb *to be* is often used.
   - They consider their son a genius.
   - I know her to be reliable.

Grammar Exercise

Arrange the following words to make full sentences.

1. At night, (nervous / driving / makes / me).

   ____

2. (hard / I / him / believe / to / be / worker / a).

   ____

3. (designed / I / the car / to / consider / badly / be).

   ____

4. (named / eldest / Joseph / son / our / we).

   ____

5. (the singer / rich / the hit song / made).

   ____

6. (teammates / made / captain / me / my).

   ____

Reading

1-31

Generally speaking, we believe that volunteers do not expect to be paid. When we think about the idea of volunteering, we think of people performing work or services for free because they have a strong desire to help others or improve the world in some way. Often, in fact, many people who volunteer already have some kind of income and do voluntary work in their free time. What is more, the kind of organizations that use volunteers, such as non-profit or community groups, do not usually have enough money to pay people.

But in certain cases, we need to accept that volunteers should receive some kind of payment for the work they do. For example, some types of volunteer work involve a long period of work, perhaps even in another country. Other types of volunteer work may need people with specialized skills, like doctors, construction experts, or engineers. A good example of this would be people volunteering to help after a natural disaster has struck, such as a typhoon or an earthquake. In cases such as these, it might be difficult to attract high-level volunteers unless some form of basic payment is offered. Generally speaking, however, such people would not receive a salary. The payment would usually be to cover travel costs and living expenses.

Perhaps it is important to understand that the word "volunteer" is not so simple. There are many situations in which volunteer work is carried out. Whether the work is paid or not will depend on the circumstances.

Vocabulary Check

Fill in the blank with words from the word box below. Change the word form if necessary.

1. For financial security, it is important that your ( ) is higher than your expenses.
2. I ( ) that I made a mistake. I'm very sorry.
3. We need technicians with ( ) skills to design the new computer system.
4. Floods, earthquakes, and typhoons are all examples of natural ( ).
5. Without offering a high salary, we cannot ( ) the most talented people.

disaster attract income specialized accept

Reading Comprehension

Answer the following questions.

1. What is our normal expectation of volunteers?

____

2. In what circumstances may specialized volunteers be necessary?

____

3. What form of payment might volunteers receive?

____

Writing

TOPIC

- What kind of volunteer work have you done or do you want to try during your time at university?

A *Write your own opinion and give at least one reason.*

____

____

B *Make pairs or groups of 3–4 people and share your ideas with each other.*

Member	Opinion and reason

C *Write down your thoughts with 2 or 3 main points, considering the opinions of your partners (around 60 words).*

____

____

____

____

____

✔ Useful Vocabulary

Category	Examples
Volunteer work	*people with disabilities, disadvantaged children, community work, environmental activities, social support*
Activities	*cleaning up, organizing trips, fund-raising, visiting hospitals*
Other	*making a contribution, improving people's lives, community building*

UNIT 7

Truths About Common Illnesses

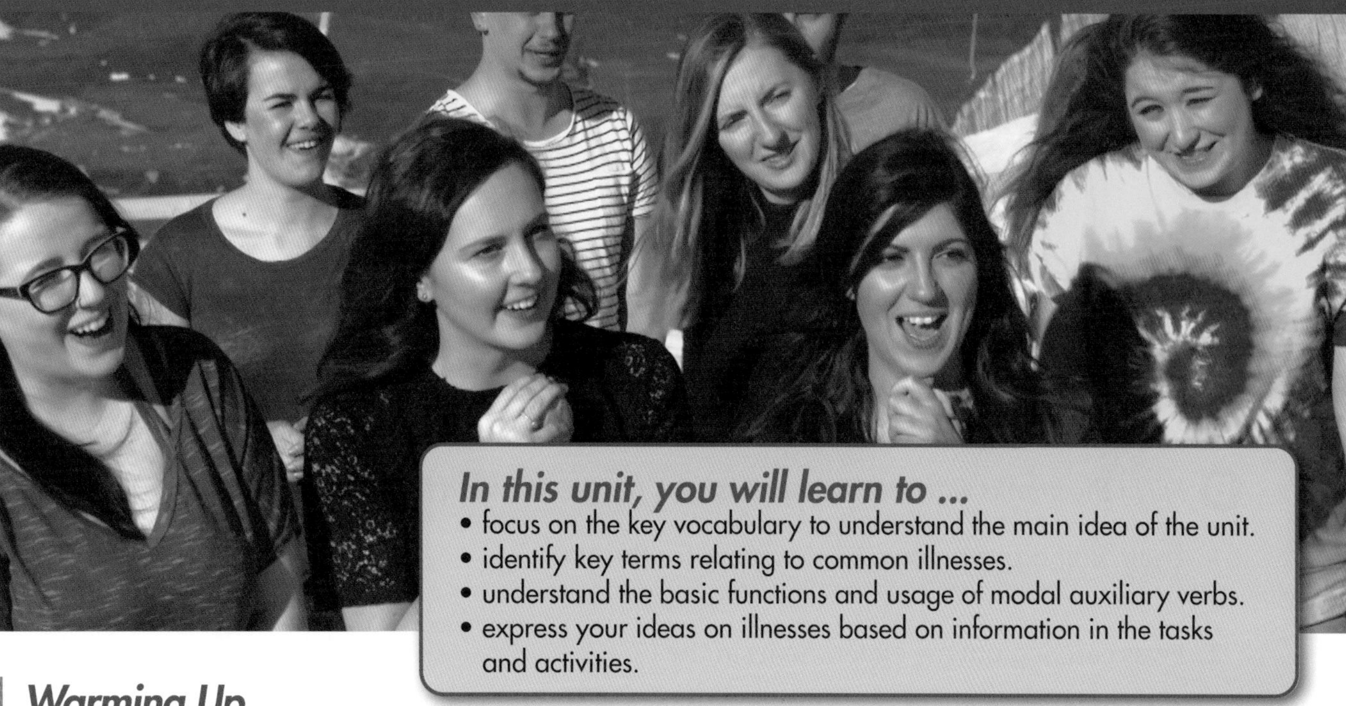

In this unit, you will learn to ...
- focus on the key vocabulary to understand the main idea of the unit.
- identify key terms relating to common illnesses.
- understand the basic functions and usage of modal auxiliary verbs.
- express your ideas on illnesses based on information in the tasks and activities.

Warming Up

Choose your own answers to the following questions. Then ask your partner the questions.

1. Which season do you like the best?

❑ Spring ❑ Summer
❑ Autumn ❑ Winter

2. When was the last time that you caught a cold?

❑ Last summer ❑ Last winter
❑ Over a year ago ❑ This season / I've got a cold now!

3. What should you do to prevent a cold?

❑ Get enough sleep ❑ Have well-balanced meals
❑ Gargle and wash hands ❑ Other (   )

Watching

WEB動画 DVD CD 1-32

Watch the video and take some notes on what you see and hear. Then, talk about your notes and the topic of the video with your partner.

illness

Vocabulary

CD 1-33

A *Match the words below with the correct explanations (a – f).*

1. cold ______
2. virus ______
3. sneeze ______
4. disease ______
5. lab ______
6. meter ______

a. an extremely small thing that causes infectious illness

b. a room or building for scientific research, experiments, testing, or analysis

c. to expel air suddenly and uncontrollably from your nose and mouth

d. a base unit for measuring length

e. an illness of humans, animals, or plants, caused by infection

f. a common illness that causes you to cough, sneeze, etc.

B *Fill in the blanks with words from Task A. Change the word form if necessary.*

1. Usain Bolt broke his own world record for the 100 (   ) twice.
2. I was carrying out my experiments in the (   ) when you called me.
3. This (   ) causes a sore throat.

Listening Comprehension

WEB動画 DVD CD 1-32

A *Watch the video again and write T if the statement is true or F if it is false.*

1. Phil thinks that people catch colds from being cold. ______
2. Javid's grandmother always says, "Make sure you're covered up. Otherwise, you'll catch a cold." ______
3. Experts advise us to exercise and wash our hands to stay healthy. ______
4. If we always cover our nose and mouth when we sneeze, we won't catch a cold from being cold. ______

B *Which number shows the correct combination of person, place, and experiment? Circle the correct number.*

	who	where	how
1	Javid	the top of a mountain	taking his coat off for 15 minutes to see whether this will result in catching a cold
2	Javid	on a bus	measuring the distance of Sally's sneeze
3	Helen	the top of a mountain	measuring the distance of Sally's sneeze
4	Helen	on a bus	taking her coat off for 15 minutes to see whether this will result in catching a cold

Tips on Listening and Speaking

 1-34

Insertion of /y/ and /w/ between Vowels

When a word or syllable ends with a tense vowel or diphthong and the next word or syllable begins with a vowel, a /y/ or /w/ sound is often inserted.

1. Can you really catch a cold from b**ei**ng cold?
2. Javid and 30 others are g**oi**ng to take their coats off at the peak of the mountain and s**ee i**f they catch colds.

Dictation

 1-35

Listen to the sentences and fill in the blanks.

1. Javid doesn't (　　　　) (　　　　) (　　　　).

2. Right, so (　　　　) (　　　　) (　　　　) (　　　　)?

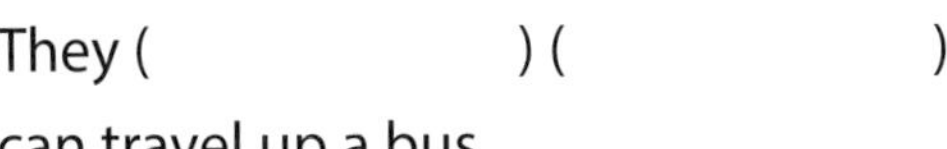

3. They (　　　　) (　　　　) (　　　　) (　　　　) the distance a sneeze can travel up a bus.

Retelling

Watch parts of the video again and tell the story of each scene to your partner. You can use the keywords below.

e.g.

Keywords

Javid, Helen and Phil, make sure, catching, true or not

Model

Javid, Helen, and Phil want to make sure whether catching a cold from being cold is true.

1.

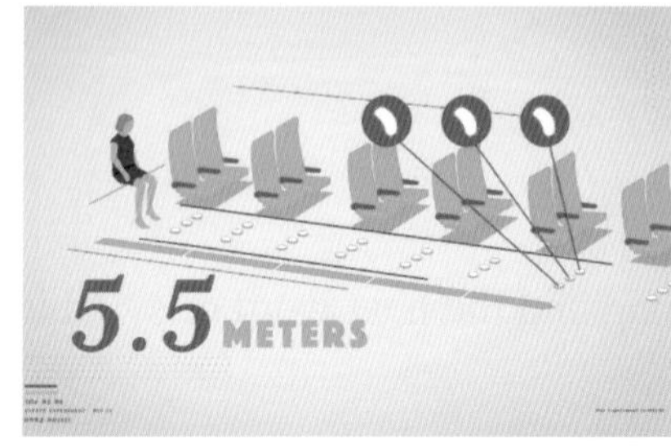

Keywords

results, experiment of Helen and Andrew, sneezes, spread, five-and-a-half meters

2.

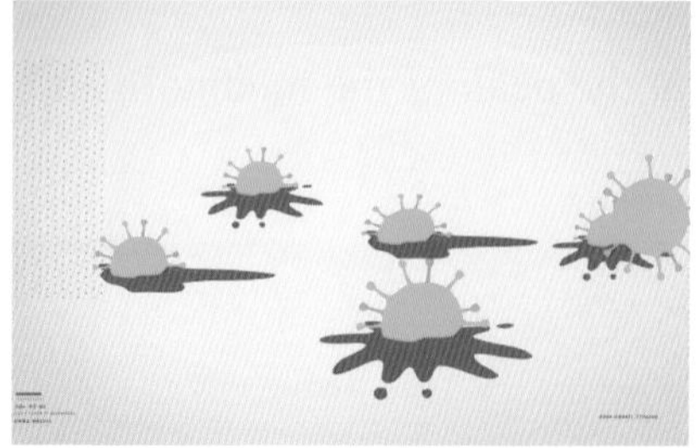

Keywords

colds and illnesses, spread, sneezes

Discussion

Q: *What is the best way to prevent a cold? Why do you think so? What do you think about your partner's ideas?*

I am afraid that is not quite true.

What's your view?

Your ideas	Your partner's ideas

Grammar

Modal Auxiliary Verbs

Modal auxiliary verbs (*can, could, shall, should, may, might, will, would, must, ought to, need to, have to*) are used with the main verb to provide extra information. Some have a past form, which is formed using *have* + past participle.

1. **Simple Modal Verbs**

Modal verbs are generally followed by the infinitive without *to*.

- You should remember your friends' birthdays.
- I must hand in my assignment tomorrow.

2. **Modal Verbs with *to***

- You ought to exercise more often.
- I have to pay my taxes this week.
- You need to get a haircut.

3. **Past Modal Verbs**

These are using *have* + past participle.

- I should have taken an earlier train.
- You might have left your wallet in the store.

Grammar Exercise

Arrange the following words to make full sentences.

1. (homework / I / you / help / your / will / do).

____

2. (should / you / studied / have / for / harder) the test.

____

3. (I / to / have / finish / report / this / by) tomorrow.

____

4. (have / that / horror / scary / must / movie / been).

____

5. (the meeting / I / late / be / to / may) today.

____

6. (to / you / take / ought / a vacation) soon.

____

Reading 1-36

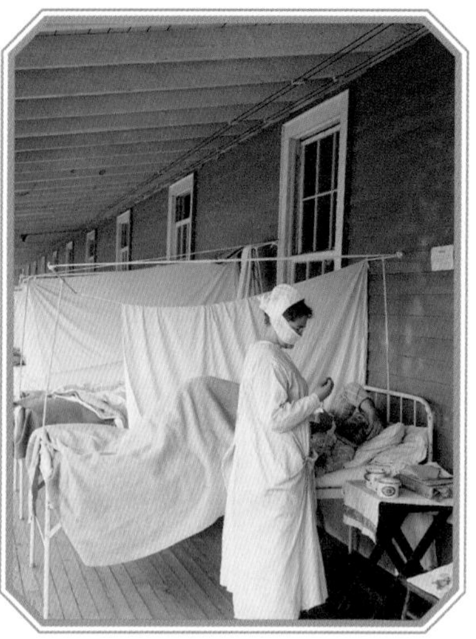

The First World War ended in November 1918. It was one of the most destructive wars the world had ever seen, killing between 15 and 23 million people. In the years immediately following the war, however, the world was hit by an even deadlier disaster, the Spanish flu pandemic, which lasted till 1920. By some estimates, the four waves of this disease infected nearly one third of the global population and killed up to 50 million people, making it one of the deadliest pandemics in human history.

Its name is misleading because we know for certain that the disease did not start in Spain. There are several theories about the country of origin, including the US, Britain, France, and China, but none of them has been generally accepted. One thing that is true, however, is that the widespread movement of large numbers of soldiers during the war probably contributed to its rapid spread.

One of the unique features of this pandemic was the age of its victims. Normally, those affected by an influenza outbreak are mostly the very young and the very old. In contrast, the Spanish flu caused many deaths among healthy young adults. In fact, it is estimated that among members of the US military, the number killed by the disease was greater than the number killed in the war. Nowadays, we are fortunate to have flu vaccines and antiviral drugs to protect us. Sadly, this was not the case in the early 20th century.

Vocabulary Check

Fill in the blank with words from the word box below. Change the word form if necessary.

1. You should wear a mask when you have flu to avoid ( ) other people.
2. The fire was extremely ( ), causing millions of dollars' worth of damage.
3. The unpopular new law caused ( ) protests across the country.
4. The ( ) of war was soon reported in the media.
5. Rapid public health measures can reduce the number of ( ).

infect	outbreak	victim	destructive	widespread

Reading Comprehension

Answer the following questions.

1. Why is the Spanish flu considered one of the deadliest pandemics in history?

____

2. Why is the name "Spanish flu" misleading?

____

3. What was unusual about the Spanish flu?

____

TOPIC

- When you feel sick, which do you prefer to take, regular medicine or herbal medicine?

A *Write your own opinion and give at least one reason.*

____

____

B *Make pairs or groups of 3–4 people and share your ideas with each other.*

Member	Opinion and reason

C *Write down your thoughts with 2 or 3 main points, considering the opinions of your partners (around 60 words).*

____

____

____

____

____

✔ Useful Vocabulary

Category	Examples
Illnesses	*cold, flu/influenza, infection*
Symptoms	*fever, rash, sore throat, headache, upset stomach*
Other	*bacteria, virus, prescription, treatment, antibiotics*

UNIT 8

Shona Faces Her Fears

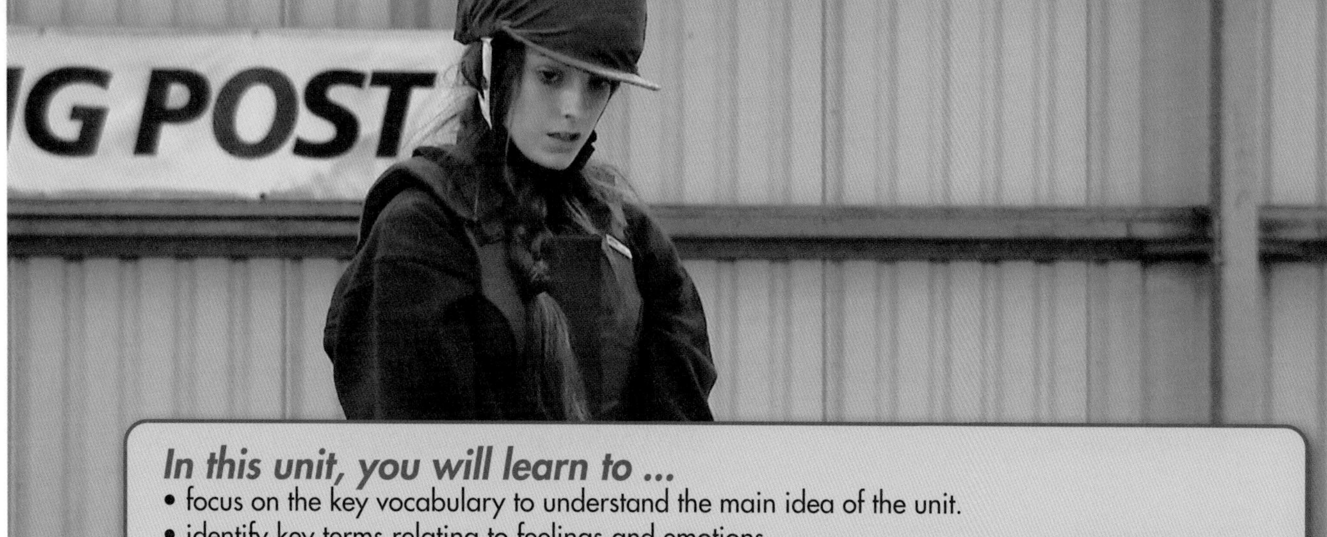

In this unit, you will learn to ...
- focus on the key vocabulary to understand the main idea of the unit.
- identify key terms relating to feelings and emotions.
- understand the basic functions and usage of the past simple, past continuous, and past perfect.
- express your ideas on feelings and emotions based on information in the tasks and activities.

Warming Up

Choose your own answers to the following questions. Then ask your partner the questions.

1. What are you afraid of?
   - ❑ Snakes
   - ❑ Injections
   - ❑ Your phone battery dying
   - ❑ Other ( )
2. What places are you afraid of?
   - ❑ Heights
   - ❑ Dark places
   - ❑ Narrow places
   - ❑ Other ( )
3. What was the scariest thing for you recently?
   - ❑ Going to the dentist
   - ❑ Watching a horror movie
   - ❑ Seeing an insect that you dislike
   - ❑ Other ( )

Watching

WEB動画 DVD CD 1-37

Watch the video and take some notes on what you see and hear. Then, talk about your notes and the topic of the video with your partner.

fear

Vocabulary

1-38

A *Match the words and phrases below with the correct explanations (a – f).*

1. nervous ______ a. feeling sure about your ability to do something well
2. frightened ______ b. feeling pleased about something you have done well
3. confident ______ c. to remain peaceful and unstressed
4. keep up ______ d. to prevent something from falling behind
5. stay calm ______ e. anxious or worried about something
6. proud ______ f. feeling fear

B *Fill in the blanks with words from Task A. Change the word form if necessary.*

1. He became (   ) in English after studying abroad in Vancouver.
2. I cannot (   ) with the rapid progress of AI.
3. I'm (   ) of large dogs even if they are gentle.

Listening Comprehension

WEB動画 DVD CD 1-37

A *Watch the video again and write T if the statement is true or F if it is false.*

1. Shona loves horses even after the fall from Gilli. ______
2. On her first day at riding school, Shona must remember how to ride a horse. ______
3. The instructor advised Shona to relax and let the horse run fast so as not to lose control. ______
4. Shona's mother is proud to hear that she went on the gallops. ______

B *Which number shows the correct combination of how Shona felt and when she felt it? Circle the correct number.*

	when	feeling
1	Before riding on the gallops	brave
2	Before riding on the gallops	worried
3	After riding on the gallops	panicked
4	After riding on the gallops	nervous

Tips on Listening and Speaking

1-39

/ŋ/

/ng/ is not two sounds, but one nasal consonant at the end of a word.

1. Everyone gets nervous or scared about thi**ng**s.
2. Shona is tryi**ng** to deal with her fear of ridi**ng** horses.
3. Before traini**ng** at ridi**ng** school, she used to worry about not bei**ng** in control and falli**ng** from the horse.

Dictation

1-40

Listen to the sentences and fill in the blanks.

1. She fell off when the horse (　　　　) (　　　　) and hurt her arm.
2. But she's (　　　　) (　　　　) (　　　　) control of the horse.
3. So just relax, (　　　　) (　　　　), (　　　　) (　　　　) great.

Retelling

WEB動画 DVD

Watch parts of the video again and tell the story of each scene to your partner. You can use the keywords below.

e.g.

Keywords

Shona, scared, frightened, cannot

Model

Shona has been scared to ride horses since she fell off two years ago. Now she is so frightened that she cannot enjoy riding.

1.

Keywords

on the first day, the instructor, not to panic, just relax

2.

Keywords

after, confident, looking, deal with her fear of

Discussion

Q: ***What should you do to deal with your fears or anxieties? Why do you think so? What do you think about your partner's ideas?***

Furthermore, …

Do you mean …?

Your ideas	Your partner's ideas

Grammar

Past Simple, Past Continuous, Past Perfect

1. Past Simple

We use this tense to describe actions that started and finished at a definite point in the past.

- I played tennis last Saturday.
- Julie met her friend last night.

2. Past Continuous

We use this tense to describe an action that was in progress at a particular point in the past.

- I was sleeping at 7 AM.
- He was watching TV when I called him.

3. Past Perfect

We use this tense to talk about an action or event that happened before another one.

- The party had (already) ended when I arrived.
- The train had (already) left when I reached the station.

Grammar Exercise

Arrange the following words to make full sentences.

1. I (he / when / left / had) called.

____

2. (university / I / graduated / years / from / two) ago.

____

3. When (the rain / stopped / woke / had / I / up,).

____

4. (married / he / July / got / in / last) year.

____

5. I (was / you / when / working / called).

____

6. She (the storm / was / when / walking / started).

____

Reading

1-41

Far fewer people are injured in airplane accidents than in car accidents. Spiders can seem scary and ugly, but with the exception of a few species, they are generally harmless. Yet, there are people who are too scared to board an airplane and those who scream when they see a spider. We say that their fears are unreasonable because they have nothing to do with the actual dangers of air travel or spiders. These fears are called phobias. Other common phobias include the fear of narrow spaces or the sight of blood.

There is another psychological condition connected to fears, known as OCD. People with this condition constantly think about a particular danger. One common example is the fear of being dirty, which makes people unwilling to touch something that another person has touched, such as a door handle. This fear may cause a person with OCD to wash their hands hundreds of times a day.

It is easy to see how phobias and OCD may affect someone's ability to lead a normal life. People may never completely lose these fears, but fortunately, there are treatments available that help people to manage these conditions. People with a fear of flying can use techniques to help them relax, such as medication or deep breathing. In another common form of treatment, a therapist will gradually expose patients to the object or situation that they fear so that they can learn to control their reactions.

Vocabulary Check

Fill in the blank with words from the word box below. Change the word form if necessary.

1. I don't like (   ) movies with ghosts or zombies.
2. Joe has visited every state in the USA with the (   ) of Alaska.
3. The bank was (   ) to give me a loan because my salary is too low.
4. The doctor gave me some (   ) to treat my sore throat.
5. There are many (   ) you have to master to become a good golfer.

exception　unwilling　technique　scary　medication

Reading Comprehension

Answer the following questions.

1. Why can a phobia be described as unreasonable?

   ____

2. What causes a person with OCD to wash their hands many times a day?

   ____

3. What are two treatments that can help people who are afraid of flying?

   ____

TOPIC

• When your friend feels nervous before a big event, how do you interact with him/her?

A *Write your own opinion and give at least one reason.*

____

____

B *Make pairs or groups of 3–4 people and share your ideas with each other.*

Member	Opinion and reason

C *Write down your thoughts with 2 or 3 main points, considering the opinions of your partners (around 60 words).*

____

____

____

____

____

✔ Useful Vocabulary

Category	Examples
Event	*sports match, speech contest, entrance exam, driving test*
Feeling	*tense, nervous, agitated, loss of self-confidence, doubt*
Other	*reassure, encourage, calm (someone) down, do deep breathing*

UNIT 9 Alternative Shopping: Vintage Markets

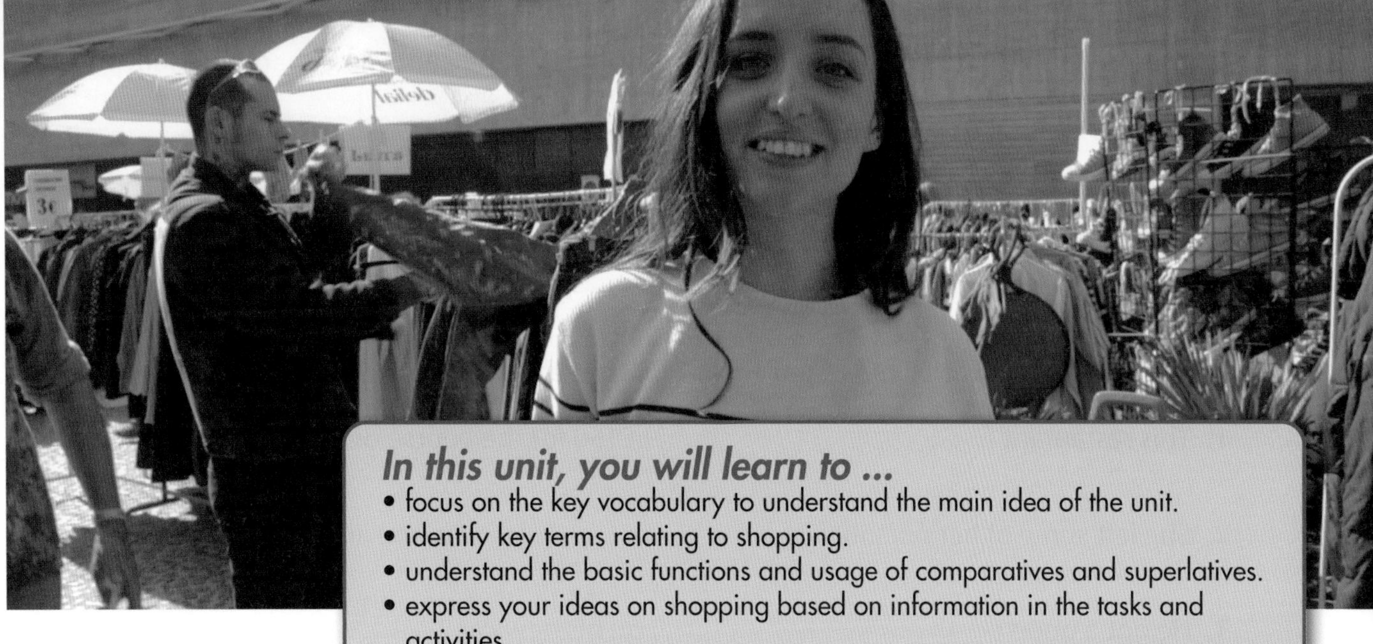

In this unit, you will learn to ...
- focus on the key vocabulary to understand the main idea of the unit.
- identify key terms relating to shopping.
- understand the basic functions and usage of comparatives and superlatives.
- express your ideas on shopping based on information in the tasks and activities.

Warming Up

Choose your own answers to the following questions. Then ask your partner the questions.

1. Which clothes do you like the best?
   - ❑ Leather jackets
   - ❑ Hoodies
   - ❑ Cardigans
   - ❑ Other (   )
2. Which pattern is the most common among the clothes you own?
   - ❑ Plain
   - ❑ Checkered/Striped
   - ❑ Floral/Animal
   - ❑ Other (   )
3. Have you ever bought clothes at a secondhand store or through an online flea market app?
   - ❑ Yes
   - ❑ No

Watching

WEB動画 DVD CD 2-01

Watch the video and take some notes on what you see and hear. Then, talk about your notes and the topic of the video with your partner.

vintage

Vocabulary

CD 2-02

A *Match the words below with the correct explanations (a – f).*

1. bargain ______
2. vendor ______
3. charge ______
4. fit ______
5. possession ______
6. deal ______

a. to require payment for goods or a service
b. an agreement, especially in business
c. something bought for significantly less than the usual price
d. a person who sells things
e. something that you have or own
f. to be the right shape and size for someone or something

B *Fill in the blanks with words from Task A. Change the word form if necessary.*

1. This restaurant (   ) €150 for the course dinner.
2. She left some of her personal (   ) in the airplane yesterday.
3. He got a good (   ) on his new car.

Listening Comprehension

A *Watch the video again and write T if the statement is true or F if it is false.*

1. Ana moved to Barcelona five years ago. ______
2. The sellers at Fleadonia Market come from not only the neighborhood. ______
3. Ana did not buy an old camera because it did not work anymore. ______
4. Two Markets is a weekly market in the north of Barcelona. ______

B *Arrange the clothes Ana looked at in the order in which they appear in the video.*

a jacket with embroidery

a dark gray jacket

a green jacket with capital "P"

a tweed jacket

a purple shirt

a brown jacket

______ ➡ ______ ➡ ______ ➡ ______ ➡ ______ ➡ ______

Tips on Listening and Speaking

2-03

Negative Form

Primary auxiliary verbs and modal verbs in a negative sentence are often stressed.

1. I love vintage shopping so I wanted to show you two of the best markets where you **can** find a lot of bargains and all kinds of things really. [unstressed]
2. With a little searching and an eye for bargains, you'll find a hidden treasure you **couldn't** find anywhere else. [stressed]

Dictation

2-04

Listen to the sentences and fill in the blanks.

1. So let's have a look around and see what we (   ) (   ).

2. It's cheap as well, 10 euros. I (   ) probably ask for less. The only problem is I (   ) (   ) if it works, but I think it's a bargain really, even if it (   ) (   ).

3. So I (   ) (   ) anything in the end because although everything is cheap, the quality (   ) really amazing.

Retelling

Watch parts of the video again and tell the story of each scene to your partner. You can use the keywords below.

e.g.

Keywords

buying and wearing, second-hand clothes, popular, the trend in fashion, now

Model

Buying and wearing second-hand clothes is now very popular and the trend in fashion.

1.

Keywords

people from the neighborhood, things they've made, buy, one-of-a-kind items

2.

Keywords

Ana, bought, Two Markets, items on sale

Discussion

Q: *What are the advantages and disadvantages of buying vintage stuff? Why do you think so? What do you think about your partner's ideas?*

May I add something at this point?

Go on, please.

Your ideas	Your partner's ideas

Grammar

Comparatives and Superlatives

There are various ways to form comparative and superlative adjectives.

1. **Adjectives of One Syllable**
   - We add *-er* or *-est,* respectively (e.g., *warm, warmer, warmest*).
2. **Spelling Considerations**
   - If the word ends in *-e*, we just add *-r* or *-st* (e.g., *nice, nicer, nicest*).
   - If the word ends in a vowel and a consonant, the consonant is doubled (e.g., *hot, hotter, hottest*).
   - If the word ends in *-y*, the *-y* becomes *-i* (e.g., *happy, happier, happiest*).
3. **Adjectives with Two or More Syllables**
   - We use *more* or *most,* respectively, before the adjective (e.g., *careful, more careful, most careful*).
   - However, please note that two-syllable adjectives ending in *-y* follow the rule in #2 above.

Grammar Exercise

Arrange the following words to make full sentences.

1. Tokyo (rainier / than / is / a / London / city).

   ____

2. (runner / I / faster / am / a / brother / my / than).

   ____

3. (difficult / is / the / subject / most / for / me) math.

   ____

4. (friend / I / a / skillful / more / skier / am / my / than).

   ____

5. (mother / is / the / person / my / happiest) I know.

   ____

6. (is / mountain / tallest / Mt. Everest / the / in) the world.

   ____

Reading

2-05

Jeans have come a long way. They were originally made to be tough pants for working men such as cowboys and farmers. Nowadays, however, jeans made by leading fashion designers such as Gucci can sell for as much as $4,000 a pair.

The man credited with inventing blue jeans was Levi Strauss, a German immigrant to the US in the 19th century. In the 1870s, he and a tailor named Jacob Davis produced denim pants with rivets, or small metal studs, to strengthen the front and back pockets. This design has remained the basic pattern for jeans ever since.

Levi Strauss

Jeans started to become a widely accepted fashion item in the 1950s, initially becoming popular among teenagers who wanted to dress entirely differently from their conservative parents. The trend continued throughout the 1960s, with jeans becoming almost a kind of uniform for hippies and other young people who were rejecting the world of the older generation.

Nowadays, you will find stores selling jeans anywhere you go in the world. However, there are some fashion-conscious people who do not want to wear ordinary mass-produced jeans. Some will pay high prices for jeans made by famous designers. Others will search in used clothing stores or online to find authentic vintage jeans, which usually cost much more than new ones.

Vocabulary Check

Fill in the blank with words from the word box below. Change the word form if necessary.

1. Computers were (   ) intended for business use rather than personal use.
2. I want to (   ) my muscles by lifting weights.
3. The building was (   ) destroyed by the huge fire.
4. (   ) people tend to spend a lot of money on clothes.
5. That restaurant serves (   ) Vietnamese dishes that taste fresh and delicious.

originally	entirely	authentic	fashion-conscious	strengthen

Reading Comprehension

Answer the following questions.

1. What kind of people were jeans originally designed for?

   ____

2. When did jeans start to become popular as a fashion item?

   ____

3. What two types of jeans may fashion-conscious people want to buy?

   ____

Writing

TOPIC

- What is the biggest issue in wearing lots of fast-fashion clothes?

A *Write your own opinion and give at least one reason.*

____

____

B *Make pairs or groups of 3–4 people and share your ideas with each other.*

Member	Opinion and reason

C *Write down your thoughts with 2 or 3 main points, considering the opinions of your partners (around 60 words).*

____

____

____

____

____

✓ Useful Vocabulary

Category	Examples
Environment	*pollution, waste, landfill, overuse of resources*
Manufacturing	*low wages, unsafe working conditions, child labor*
Other	*environmental awareness, three "R's"*

UNIT 10

Can a Computer Write a Musical?

In this unit, you will learn to ...

- focus on the key vocabulary to understand the main idea of the unit.
- identify key terms relating to computers and theatrical activities.
- understand the basic functions and usage of relative pronouns.
- express your ideas on various uses of computers based on information in the tasks and activities.

Warming Up

Choose your own answers to the following questions. Then ask your partner the questions.

1. Which devices do you usually use?
   - ❑ Smartphone
   - ❑ Laptop PC
   - ❑ Tablet
   - ❑ Other ( )
2. For what purposes do you use the above devices?
   - ❑ Browsing the Internet
   - ❑ Watching movies
   - ❑ Communicating with friends
   - ❑ Other ( )
3. What kind of movies or musicals do you prefer?
   - ❑ Fantasy
   - ❑ Comedy
   - ❑ Romance
   - ❑ Other ( )

Watching

WEB動画 DVD CD 2-06

Watch the video and take some notes on what you see and hear. Then, talk about your notes and the topic of the video with your partner.

musicals

Vocabulary

CD 2-07

A *Match the words below with the correct explanations (a – f).*

1. theater ______
2. audience ______
3. experiment ______
4. tune ______
5. fabulous ______
6. prove ______

a. a group or large gathering of people who watch a performance
b. an attempt to see if something new or different works well
c. extremely good or impressive
d. a building or place where plays and shows are performed
e. a series of musical tones that are usually attractive and memorable
f. to show that something is true or viable by providing evidence, examples, etc.

B *Fill in the blanks with words from Task A. Change the word form if necessary.*

1. The kids were playing a popular ( ) on the old piano.
2. We encourage ( ) participation during our show.
3. The president explained Brazil's unique ( ) with alcohol-powered cars.

Listening Comprehension

WEB動画 DVD CD 2-06

A *Watch the video again and write T if the statement is true or F if it is false.*

1. Their project was not the first computer-generated musical. ______
2. People love stories with adventures, mysteries, and a happy ending. ______
3. Alex and James are performers in West End theater shows. ______
4. Nathan considered the possibility that the musical would fail. ______

B ***Which number is the right combination of the characters and what they do? Circle the correct number.***

	Characters	What they do
1	Benjamin and Nathan	create lyrics
2	Nathan and Neil	collect data
3	Benjamin and Nathan	decide the story
4	Benjamin and Luke	create music

Tips on Listening and Speaking

 2-08

Linking Consonant to Vowel

When a word ends with a consonant and the next word begins with a vowel, these two sounds are linked.

1. Each show is made by talented teams who work together to create enjoyable songs, exciting music **and‿an‿unforgettable** story.
2. Every decision we make needs to come back to the **sets‿of** data that **got‿us there‿in** the first place.
3. Every **time‿I run‿it**, we get **back‿a** totally different tune.

Dictation

 2-09

Listen to the sentences and fill in the blanks.

1. Benjamin and Nathan go to a university ( ) ( ) ( ) find out what computers think makes a good story.

2. Benjamin and Nick must continue searching through the computer's music to find some that is ( ) ( ) ( ) use.

3. Computers might not ( ) ( ) ( ) write every West End show, but this experiment proves that with ( ) ( ) imagination — and ( ) ( ) ( ) hard work — anything is possible.

Retelling

Watch parts of the video again and tell the story of each scene to your partner. You can use the keywords below.

e.g.

Keywords

have created, musicals, years, starting, computer, whether, can, also

Model

Benjamin, Nathan, Neil, and Luke have created musicals and been successful for years. They are trying to find out whether a computer can also create a good musical.

1.

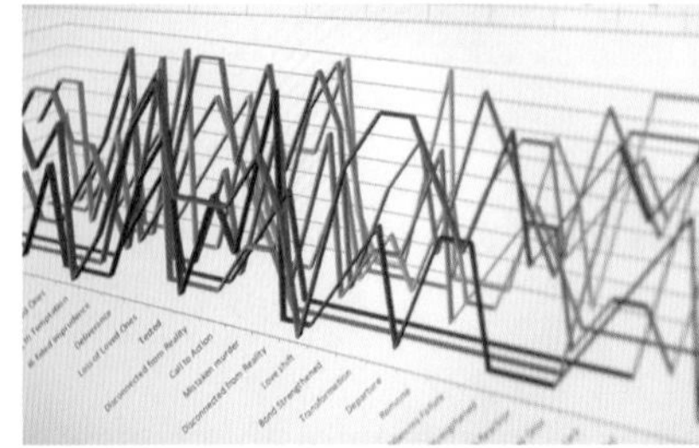

Keywords

data, audiences, favorite, challenges, love, happy ending

2.

Keywords

software, writes, single letters

Discussion

Q: *Do you agree that computers can create impressive musicals? Why do you think so? What do you think about your partner's ideas?*

In my opinion, …

I (dis)agree with you.

Your ideas	Your partner's ideas

Grammar

Relative Pronouns

Relative clauses can begin with the pronouns *who, that, which, or whose.*

1. ***Who* can be used only with people.**
   - I have a friend ***who*** can speak five languages.
   - I know someone ***who*** is an expert at fixing computer problems.

2. ***That* is mostly used for things but can also refer to people.**
   - The producers of the show used a program ***that*** can write music.
   - I have a friend ***that*** can speak five languages.

3. ***Which* is only used for things, never for people.**
   - The producers of the show used a program ***which*** can write music.
   - I usually eat lunch at a restaurant ***which*** serves vegetarian food.

4. ***Whose* is used when referring to possession.**
   - That's the girl ***whose*** father is a famous actor.
   - I'd like to find the person ***whose*** car is blocking my driveway.

Grammar Exercise

Arrange the words to make full sentences.

1. The bread (bought / I / delicious / yesterday / was / that).

   ____

2. She is (a woman / well-known / achievements / are / whose).

   ____

3. The person (I / old / met / was / an / who / classmate).

   ____

4. The bus (that / I / minutes / every / took / runs / 30).

   ____

5. (is / whose / he / a writer / sold / books / have) incredibly well.

   ____

6. I met (someone / Chinese / that / speak / can / fluent).

   ____

Reading

ANALYSIS OF EMOTIONS

CD 2-10

One of the most common everyday uses of AI is voice detection. This feature allows digital assistants such as Apple's Siri or Amazon's Alexa to understand instructions and react accordingly by answering questions, composing messages, or setting reminders. But as a result of recent technological advances, there is evidence that AI can understand not only our speech but also our emotions. It does this by analyzing the subtle changes in facial expressions that indicate how we are feeling.

This is known as emotion recognition technology, or ERT, and its uses are growing. One obvious field of application is market research, as it enables companies to test people's reactions to things such as a new breakfast cereal or to the content of a movie. Other uses, however, are more controversial. These include its growing use in job interviews, in which it can scan interviewees' faces to identify reactions or personal characteristics. This is often done without the interviewees' knowledge or consent. It can also be applied for security purposes, especially at airports, to detect signs of dishonesty or nervousness.

One important criticism of the technology is that the basic theory may not be fully supported by scientific evidence. The theory of "basic emotions" maintains that human beings across the world express emotions in the same way regardless of their cultural background. Recent research in anthropology, however, has shown that this is not necessarily true. Even though ERT appears to be a major breakthrough, more research is needed before its results can be completely trusted.

Vocabulary Check

Fill in the blank with words from the word box below. Change the word form if necessary.

1. Yesterday, Tom ( ) the data in order to find a solution to the problem.
2. The ( ) new tax has made many people angry.
3. I need my parents' ( ) to take part in the overseas study program.
4. The event on Sunday will go ahead ( ) of the weather.
5. The scientists won an award for their ( ) in genetic technology.

consent	analyze	regardless	breakthrough	controversial

Reading Comprehension

Answer the following questions.

1. How can AI detect people's emotions?

____

____

2. In what ways are some companies using emotion recognition technology?

____

____

3. What has recent research in anthropology shown?

____

____

TOPIC

- What kind of jobs will AI never replace?

A *Write your own opinion and give at least one reason.*

____

____

B *Make pairs or groups of 3–4 people and share your ideas with each other.*

Member	Opinion and reason

C *Write down your thoughts with 2 or 3 main points, considering the opinions of your partners (around 60 words).*

____

____

____

____

____

✔ Useful Vocabulary

Category	Examples
Jobs	*translator, copywriter, computer programmer, accountant*
Types of work	*manual labor, design, creative writing, data analysis*
Other	*creativity, design, feedback, interaction, strength, weakness*

UNIT 11 Reaching for the Stars

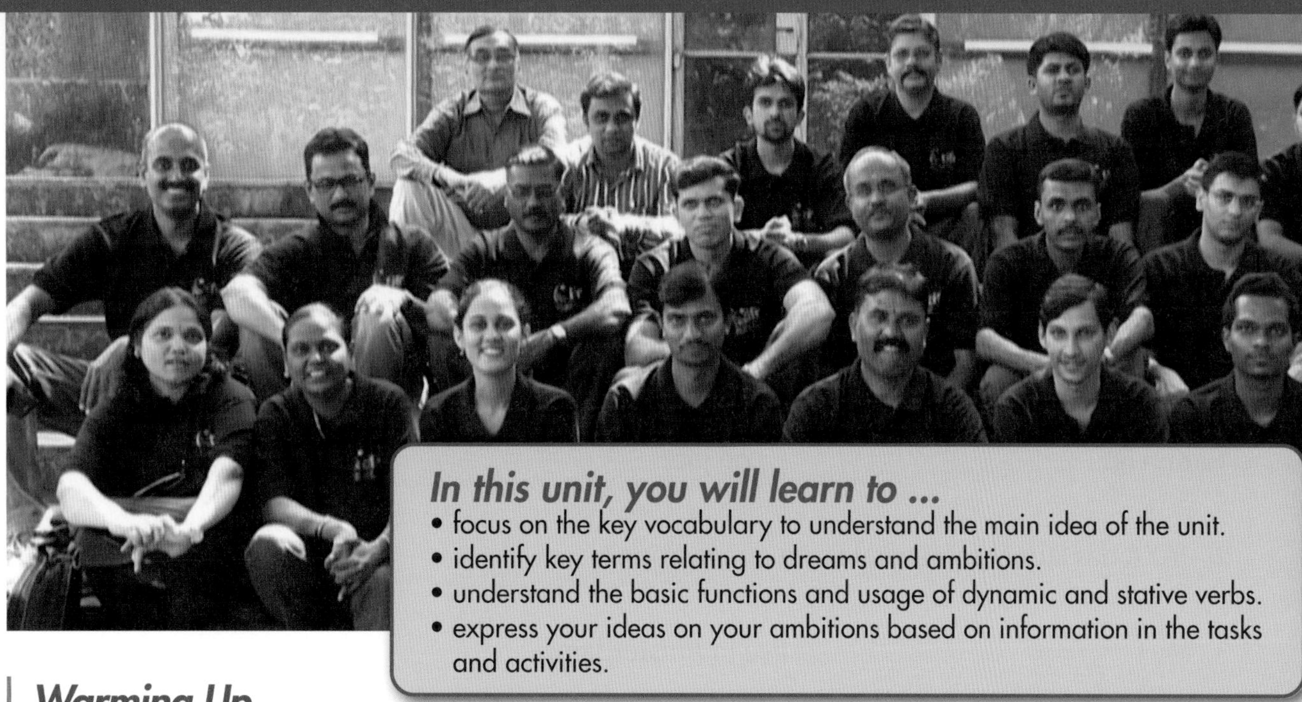

In this unit, you will learn to ...
- focus on the key vocabulary to understand the main idea of the unit.
- identify key terms relating to dreams and ambitions.
- understand the basic functions and usage of dynamic and stative verbs.
- express your ideas on your ambitions based on information in the tasks and activities.

Warming Up

Choose your own answers to the following questions. Then ask your partner the questions.

1. What did you dream of becoming as a child?
   - ❑ An athlete
   - ❑ A pastry chef
   - ❑ A singer
   - ❑ Other ( )
2. What is your favorite subject?
   - ❑ Physics
   - ❑ Arts
   - ❑ Foreign languages
   - ❑ Other ( )
3. How long do you spend studying your worst subject?
   - ❑ 30 minutes a day or more
   - ❑ 1 hour a day
   - ❑ 2 hours a day or more
   - ❑ Less than 30 minutes a day

Watching

WEB動画 DVD CD 2-11

Watch the video and take some notes on what you see and hear. Then, talk about your notes and the topic of the video with your partner.

dreams

Vocabulary

CD 2-12

A *Match the words and phrases below with the correct explanations (a – f).*

1. settle down ______
2. satellite ______
3. astronomy ______
4. institution ______
5. keen ______
6. relative ______

a. the scientific study of planets, stars, etc.
b. a device that is sent into space and moves around the Earth
c. very interested in someone or something
d. to start to live a steady life in one place, often with a partner
e. a large organization that has a particular purpose
f. a person in the same family

B *Fill in the blanks with words from Task A. Change the word form if necessary.*

1. Kim is ( ) on jazz.
2. JAXA has launched several Earth observation ( ) into orbit.
3. My ( ) live in Amsterdam.

Listening Comprehension

WEB動画 DVD CD 2-11

A *Watch the video again and write T if the statement is true or F if it is false.*

1. Vinita has wanted to be an astronomer since she heard a news that an Indian institution successfully sent a satellite into space when she was 15 years old. ______
2. Vinita wants to be in Mumbai because the only institution where research into the universe is happening is there. ______
3. Vinita is too busy with her research to go on dates. ______
4. Vinita's mother wants her to get married as soon as possible. ______

B ***What social expectation from relatives is Vinita is facing? Check the correct answers in the box below.***

☐	working in the field of astronomy	☐	earning a lot of money
☐	having a family	☐	skipping men whom she does not like
☐	finding out how the universe was formed	☐	settling down

Tips on Listening and Speaking

 2-13

Sentence Stress

Content words are stressed (i.e., strong vowels are pronounced more clearly and longer) in a sentence.

1. She is one of the **scientists** to **work** on **sending** **India's** **first** **satellite** into **space**.
2. **Sometimes**, she **goes** on **dates** that her **parents** have **arranged**.

Dictation

 2-14

Listen to the sentences and fill in the blanks.

1. Society has its expectations, but for now, Vinita ( ) ( ) ( ) into science.
2. And she's ( ) ( ) ( ) something great.
3. ( ) ( ) ( ) Vinita, these girls know they can reach for the stars.

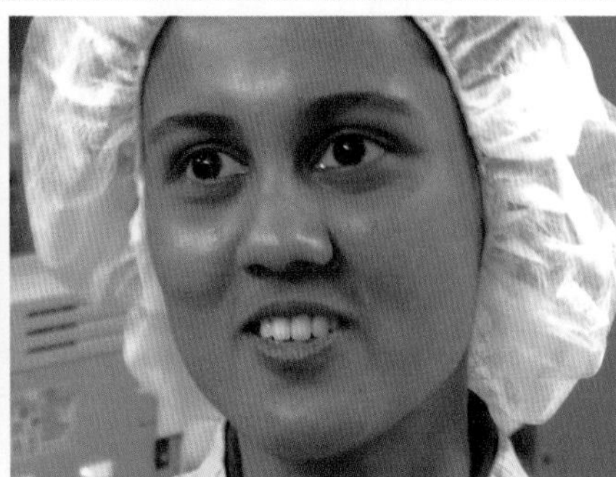

Retelling

Watch parts of the video again and tell the story of each scene to your partner. You can use the keywords below.

e.g.

Keywords

Vinita, she, few, study astronomy

Model

Vinita is happy because she is one of few women who study astronomy.

1.

Keywords

Vinita's mother, her relatives, when, over and over

2.

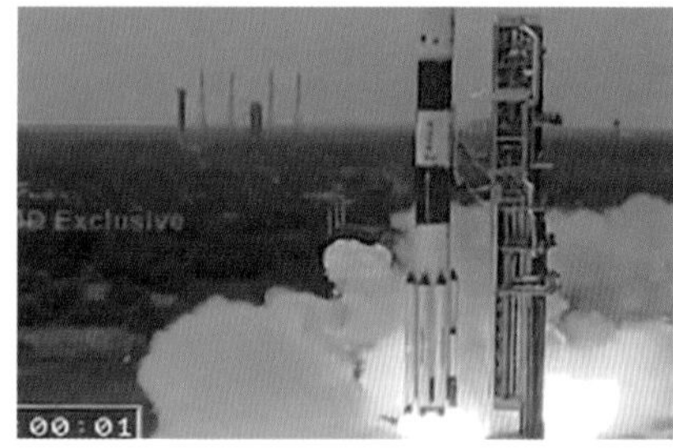

Keywords

her study, will contribute, understanding, universe

Discussion

Q: *How should society be changed so that children can make their dreams come true? Why do you think so? What do you think about your partner's ideas?*

As far as I am concerned …

I take a different view.

Your ideas	Your partner's ideas

Grammar

Dynamic Verbs and Stative Verbs

1. Dynamic Verbs

They describe actions (*run, walk, eat,* etc.), events (*happen, occur,* etc.), or processes (*grow, develop,* etc.). They are commonly used in the continuous form.

2. Stative Verbs

They describe a state or condition. They are less common and not usually used in the continuous form. They express:

- Thoughts and opinions (*agree, believe, know, remember,* etc.).
- Feelings and emotions (*like, love, hate, prefer, want,* etc.).
- Senses and perceptions (*appear, feel, be, look, see, hear, smell, taste,* etc.).
- Possession (*have, belong, own,* etc.).

3. Stative/Dynamic Verbs

Some verbs can be used both as stative and dynamic verbs.

- I see a bird in the sky (S); I'm seeing my friends tomorrow (D)
- I think this is correct (S); I'm thinking about the exams (D)

Grammar Exercise

Arrange the following words to make full sentences.

1. (ate / I / dinner / with / parents / my) yesterday.

____

2. (sick / I / a / feeling / little / am) today.

____

3. (has / playing / two / been / tennis / he / for) hours.

____

4. (meeting / I / year / remember / person / that / last).

____

5. (is / dentist / the / seeing / tomorrow / he) afternoon.

____

6. (cake / birthday / tasted / my / delicious).

____

Reading

2-15

India has always produced talented mathematicians and scientists. In fact, it was Indian mathematicians who introduced the concept of zero into mathematics. In the field of IT, however, the United States became the home of innovation, while India's role was to supply large numbers of expert engineers. India's IT companies were hired by US clients to provide services such as writing software code. India was perfect for tasks such as these. For one thing, it had a huge number of talented engineers whose salaries were lower than those of US engineers. For another, the large time difference between India and the US meant that Indian companies would be hard at work while their US clients were asleep.

Nowadays, though, India has emerged from this secondary role to become one of the world's leading innovators in the IT field. The city of Bengaluru (previously Bangalore) is the main center, containing around 40 percent of India's IT industry. Bengaluru is beginning to resemble California's Silicon Valley as a dynamic technology center, with start-up companies growing at almost the fastest rate in the world.

India's ambition to become one of the world's leading technological powers goes beyond IT. It also extends to other fields such as space exploration. One major step along this path occurred in August 2023, when India became only the fourth country to land a spacecraft on the Moon, following the US, the former Soviet Union, and China.

Vocabulary Check

Fill in the blank with words from the word box below. Change the word form if necessary.

1. The (   ) of gods is found in every human society.

2. Only the most (   ) dancers were successful in passing the audition.

3. Japan (   ) as a major economic power in the 1970s.

4. Sally is a (   ) businessperson with lots of energy.

5. After a successful launch, the (   ) is now orbiting Earth.

concept	spacecraft	emerge	talented	dynamic

Reading Comprehension

Answer the following questions.

1. Which two factors made India suitable as a partner for American IT companies?

   ____

2. In what way is Bengaluru a dynamic technology center?

   ____

3. Which countries have succeeded in landing a spacecraft on the Moon?

   ____

TOPIC

- What kind of job do you want to do in the future?

A *Write your own opinion and give at least one reason.*

B *Make pairs or groups of 3–4 people and share your ideas with each other.*

Member	Opinion and reason

C *Write down your thoughts with 2 or 3 main points, considering the opinions of your partners (around 60 words).*

✔ Useful Vocabulary

Category	Examples
Jobs	*scientist, doctor, lawyer, designer, teacher, researcher, accountant*
Professional areas	*law, education, science and technology, media, management, publishing, creative industries, advertising, PR*
Other	*aim for, ambition, work toward, internship, professional qualifications*

UNIT 12

Bionic Hand

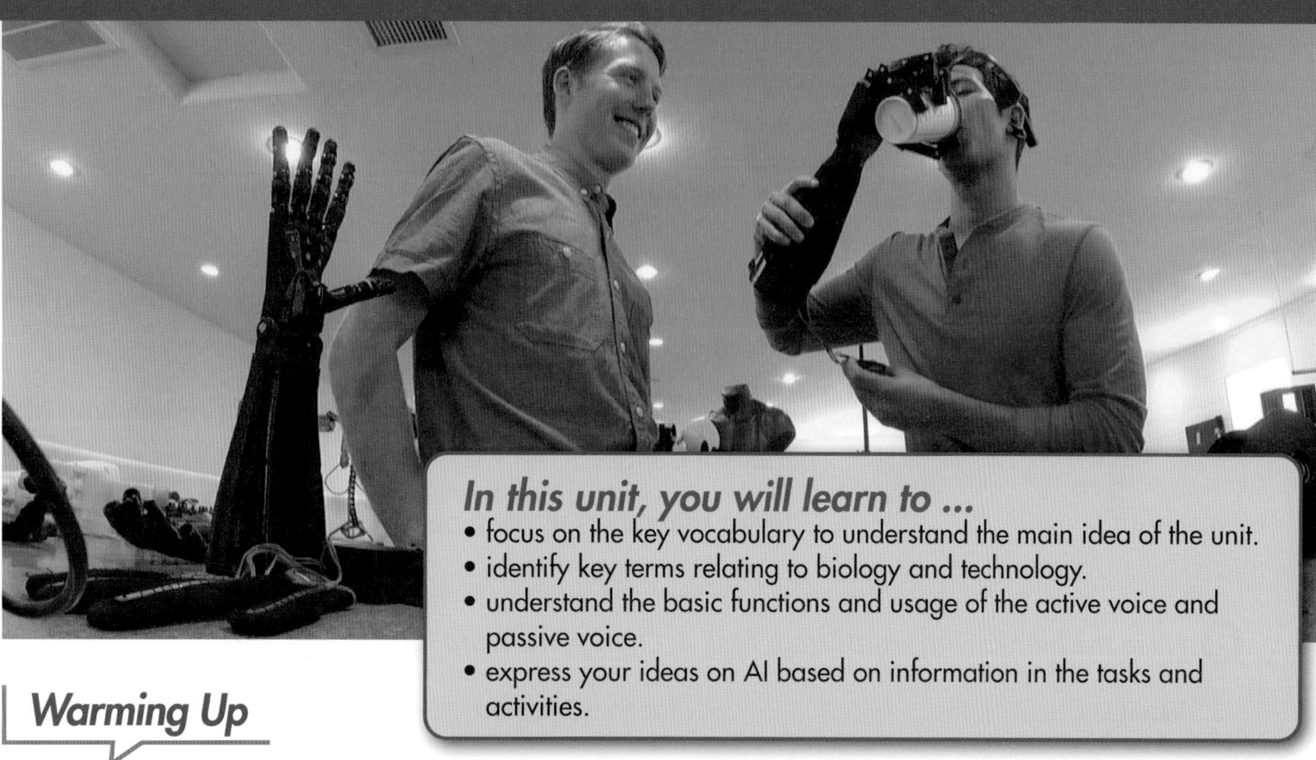

In this unit, you will learn to ...

- focus on the key vocabulary to understand the main idea of the unit.
- identify key terms relating to biology and technology.
- understand the basic functions and usage of the active voice and passive voice.
- express your ideas on AI based on information in the tasks and activities.

Warming Up

Choose your own answers to the following questions. Then ask your partner the questions.

1. How do you look up a word you do not know?
   - ❑ By using a paper dictionary
   - ❑ By using an electronic dictionary
   - ❑ By using an online dictionary
   - ❑ By asking your teacher or friend
2. Do you know about any of the robots listed below?
   - ❑ Rescue robots
   - ❑ Nursing care robots
   - ❑ Delivery robots
   - ❑ Other (   )
3. What kind of AI technology have you used?
   - ❑ Translation
   - ❑ Cleaning
   - ❑ Voice assistant
   - ❑ Other (   )

Watching

WEB動画 DVD CD 2-16

Watch the video and take some notes on what you see and hear. Then, talk about your notes and the topic of the video with your partner.

3D printer

Vocabulary

CD 2-17

A *Match the words below with the correct explanations (a – f).*

1. robotic ______
2. prototype ______
3. sensor ______
4. muscle ______
5. basis ______
6. control ______

a. the first form or model of something from which later forms are developed

b. relating to machines that can carry out complex actions automatically

c. body tissue that can tighten and relax to move a part of the body

d. the important facts, ideas, or events from which something can be developed

e. the power to make decisions about the actions or behavior of people or things

f. a device that reacts to light, heat, movement, etc.

B *Fill in the blanks with words from Task A. Change the word form if necessary.*

1. What is the ( ) for this decision?
2. The ( ) of the new car is fully autonomous.
3. Move inside, Ady! The ( ) is keeping the doors open.

Listening Comprehension

WEB動画 DVD CD 2-16

A *Watch the video again and write T if the statement is true or F if it is false.*

1. Easton is world-famous as the creator of robotic hands. ______
2. Easton is an old friend of Justin's, so Justin knows when and how Easton creates his robotic hands. ______
3. At first, Easton tried to create his robotic hands with household items. ______
4. A 3D printer makes it possible to manufacture the hand more inexpensively. ______

B *Check the body part a person with no hand can use to control the third prototype of the robotic hand?*

☐ 

☐ 

☐ 

☐ 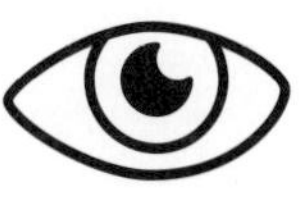

Tips on Listening and Speaking

 2-18

Stress Pattern

In compound nouns, the first elements tend to receive more stress.

1. Today, Justin meets inventor and **businessman**, Easton LaChappelle. [BUSINESSman]
2. His next goal was to find a way of making the hand available to **everybody**. [EVERYbody]

Dictation

 2-19

Listen to the sentences and fill in the blanks.

1. And it was equipped with ( ) and sensors from his own remote-controlled ( ).
2. He used a ( ) that told the robotic hand what to do by reading muscle movements and ( ).
3. If he raises his ( ), the hand opens.

Retelling

WEB動画 DVD

Watch parts of the video again and tell the story of each scene to your partner. You can use the keywords below.

e.g.

Keywords

Easton, first, materials, such as

Model

Easton made the first prototype with simple materials such as electrical tubing, fishing line, and Lego bricks.

1.

Keywords

succeeded in, help, develop, prosthetic hand

2.

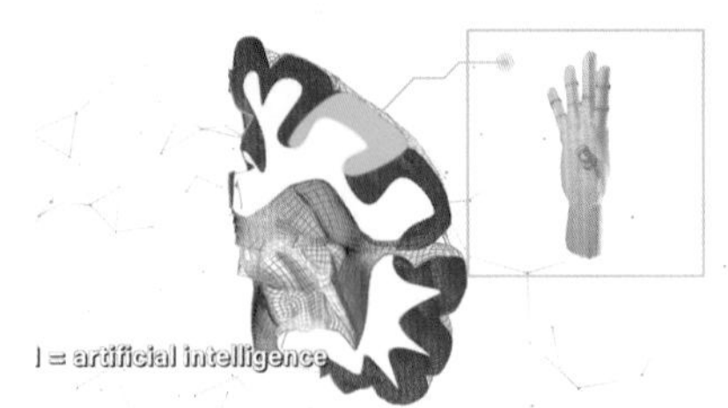

Keywords

prosthetic hand, AI system, movements, often

Discussion

Q: What kind of AI robot do you want to have the most? Why do you think so? What do you think about your partner's ideas?

To sum up, …

Sorry, I didn't catch that.

Your ideas	Your partner's ideas

Grammar

Active and Passive Voices

1. Active Voice

Verbs in the active voice are by far the most common types of verb in English. They emphasize the subject (or the "doer" of the action).

- The dog bit the man.
- The student wrote an essay.

2. Passive Voice

The passive voice is much less common in English. It tends to emphasize the object of the action.

- The man was bitten by the dog.
- The essay was written by the student.

In general, the active voice should be used wherever possible because it is clearer and more direct.

3. Passive with "get"

Generally speaking, the passive is formed using the verb *be* + past participle. Occasionally we can use the verb *get* instead of the verb *be*.

- My car got stolen.
- The cup got broken.

Grammar Exercise

Arrange the following words to make full sentences.

1. (car / damaged / last / my / got) week.

____

2. (cleaned / the / in / workers / the / windows) the office.

____

3. I (sent /grandparents / the letter / my / to).

____

4. (dinner / prepared / was / the / by) the chef.

____

5. (got / house / destroyed / the / in) the earthquake.

____

6. (painted / the picture / was / by / my) father.

____

Reading

2-20

As human beings, we have our skeletons inside our bodies. But what if we also had a skeleton on the outside? Creating robotic external skeletons, or exoskeletons, for humans has become an exciting area of research. One purpose of a robotic exoskeleton would be to increase human strength. We can imagine such devices helping workers to lift and move heavy objects.

Another, and perhaps more important, area for applying such devices is in the field of physical therapy. Researchers are making progress in designing devices that can imitate the movements of the human body. For example, there are now robotic exoskeletons that can help people with disabilities or stroke victims regain the ability to move more freely.

One disadvantage is cost. Such advanced exoskeleton devices can cost as much as $80,000. There are, however, companies that are trying to make them cheaper. One such company, based in the US, is called suitX. It manufactures a lower-body robotic exoskeleton for around $30,000. It is designed to allow people with severe physical problems to get up out of a wheelchair and walk. This is a great breakthrough for such people. On the one hand, the ability to move around relatively freely and accomplish daily tasks gives them a much-improved quality of life. On the other hand, the psychological benefits are also huge. Normally, wheelchair users must wait for someone to approach them before they can interact. The ability to rise from a wheelchair and approach others independently can be an enormous boost to their self-confidence.

Vocabulary Check

Fill in the blank with words from the word box below. Change the word form if necessary.

1. In the museum, we saw the ( ) of a huge dinosaur.
2. Ken always makes us laugh when he ( ) our teacher's voice.
3. I had a car accident, but luckily, the damage was not ( ).
4. The friendly dog ( ) me and sniffed my hand.
5. Traveling through Europe alone gave me more ( ).

skeleton self-confidence severe imitate approach

Reading Comprehension

Answer the following questions.

1. What are two ways in which robotic exoskeletons can help people?

   ____

2. What is one disadvantage of robotic exoskeletons?

   ____

3. Why are robotic exoskeletons good for people who use wheelchairs?

   ____

TOPIC

- Do you think AI is capable of creating funny jokes?

A *Write your own opinion and give at least one reason.*

____

____

B *Make pairs or groups of 3–4 people and share your ideas with each other.*

Member	Opinion and reason

C *Write down your thoughts with 2 or 3 main points, considering the opinions of your partners (around 60 words).*

____

____

____

____

____

✔ Useful Vocabulary

Category	Examples
Types of humor	*pun, play on words, one-liner, comedy monologue, comedy sketch, punchline*
Technology	*artificial general intelligence, conversational AI, chatbot, natural language generation*
Other	*sense of humor, make someone laugh*

UNIT 13

Life Afloat

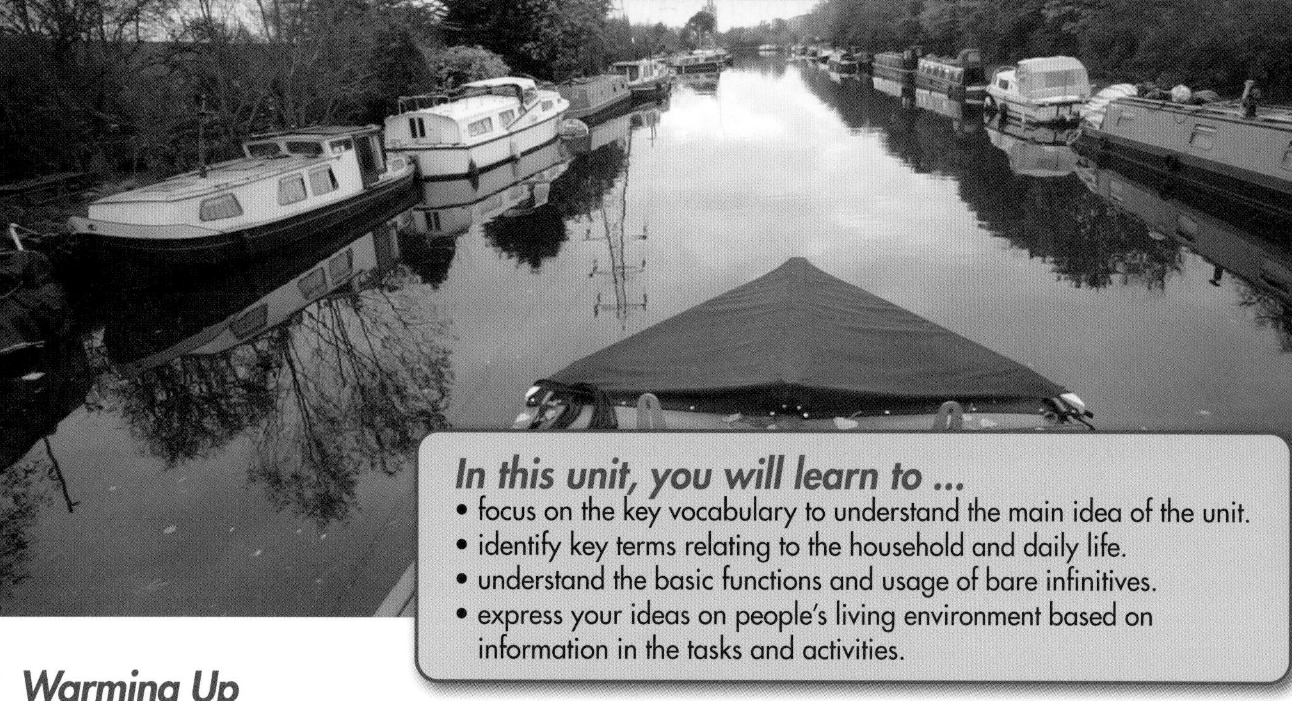

In this unit, you will learn to ...

- focus on the key vocabulary to understand the main idea of the unit.
- identify key terms relating to the household and daily life.
- understand the basic functions and usage of bare infinitives.
- express your ideas on people's living environment based on information in the tasks and activities.

Warming Up

Choose your own answers to the following questions. Then ask your partner the questions.

1. Where do you prefer to live?
   - ❑ Urban area
   - ❑ Suburban area
   - ❑ Rural area
   - ❑ Other (   )
2. Where do you prefer to spend your vacation?
   - ❑ In the mountains
   - ❑ By the beach
   - ❑ At the lake
   - ❑ Other (   )
3. When you travel, which means of transportation do you frequently use?
   - ❑ Bullet train
   - ❑ Plane
   - ❑ Bus
   - ❑ Other (   )

Watching

Watch the video and take some notes on what you see and hear. Then, talk about your notes and the topic of the video with your partner.

boat

Vocabulary 2-22

A *Match the words below with the correct explanations (a – f).*

1. escape ______ a. a space in which something can be kept
2. canal ______ b. a long and thin passage of water for boats to travel along
3. solution ______ c. to sail along or over an area of water
4. storage ______ d. a way of solving a problem or dealing with a difficult situation
5. narrow ______ e. to get away from or avoid something unpleasant or dangerous
6. navigate ______ f. measuring a small distance from one side to the other

B *Fill in the blanks with words from Task A. Change the word form if necessary.*

1. These two companies sought an acceptable (   ) to the conflict between them.
2. The Seven Seas Mariner (   ) the North Pacific.
3. Our baby will soon be born, so we need more (   ) in our bedroom.

Listening Comprehension WEB動画 DVD CD 2-21

A *Watch the video again and write T if the statement is true or F if it is false.*

1. Andrea and Greg are artists, and Fig is their dog. ______
2. Andrea and Greg decided to live on a canal boat because it cost too much to live in the city center. ______
3. There are no traffic jams on the river. ______
4. Andrea and Greg do not have to break their journey for the night because they can travel along the river while sleeping. ______

B *What does the houseboat in the video have? Choose all the collect answers in the below.*

☐ closet

☐ bathroom

☐ bedroom

☐ kitchen

☐ nursery

☐ workout room

Tips on Listening and Speaking

 2-23

Rising Intonation

Rising intonation shows an unfinish thought or uncertainty. It is usually used with questions but not with WH-Qs because WH-Qs are not real questions but requests for information.

1. Meet **Andrea** (↗), **Greg** (↗), and Fig (↘).
2. **So** (↗), a houseboat on the canal was the perfect solution (↘).

Dictation

 2-24

Listen to the sentences and fill in the blanks.

1. (　　　　) (　　　　) (　　　　), Fig loves it!
2. But (　　　　) (　　　　) (　　　　) (　　　　)?
3. It isn't (　　　　) (　　　　) (　　　　), but as Andrea says, when you live on the river, (　　　　) you have to go with the flow.

Retelling

Watch parts of the video again and tell the story of each scene to your partner. You can use the keywords below.

e.g.

Keywords

big city, before, troubled, urban pollution

Model

Greg and Andrea lived in a big city but were troubled by the urban pollution there.

1.

Keywords

advantage, sure, park their boat, available space

2.

Keywords

the side of the canal, crowded, space, gate

Discussion

Q: ***If you lived in a tiny house like Andrea and Greg, what is the minimum you would need to stay healthy and enjoy cultural activities? Why do you think so? What do you think about your partner's ideas?***

There's no doubt in my mind that …

Sorry to interrupt, but …

Your ideas	Your partner's ideas

Grammar

Bare Infinitives

Usually the infinitive form in English contains the word "to" (e.g., *to work, to play, to live*). Sometimes, however, "to" is omitted. This type of infinitive is known as a bare infinitive (also base form). Bare infinitives are found in the following cases.

1. **After Modal Verbs**
   - You should see a doctor.
   - I must call my friend.
2. **After the Object of Some Causative Verbs**
   - The teacher had me write an essay.
   - My parents made me go to bed early.
3. **After "Would Rather" and "Had Better"**
   - I would rather see a movie.
   - You had better leave soon.
4. **After the Object of Verbs of Perception**
   - We saw a cat jump onto the table.
   - I heard someone call my name.

Grammar Exercise

Arrange the following words to make full sentences.

1. (watched / I / the airplane / off / take).

____

2. (drink / I / rather / coffee / would) than tea.

____

3. (she / confidently / speak / in / can) public.

____

4. (made / car / me / the police officer / move / my).

____

5. (should / eat / we / dinner) soon.

____

6. (me / the teacher / leave / let / early / class).

____

Reading

2-25

If you take a walk along one of London's many canals, you will immediately be struck by the many houseboats moored in almost every available space. In the past, most of them were used for leisure: people would rent them for a weekend or for a relaxing summer vacation. Nowadays, however, you are more likely to find that many of these boats serve as a permanent home for all kinds of people.

These days, the reasons for choosing to live on a houseboat are economic rather than romantic. London's cost of living is among the highest in the world. Even a one-room apartment in a not-very-fashionable part of the city could cost as much as ¥150,000 per month. What is more, economic factors such as inflation are pushing energy and food costs higher and higher. Even young professionals such as doctors and lawyers are struggling to pay their monthly bills.

Switching from a regular apartment to a houseboat offers a much cheaper way to live. Used boats can be bought for a little over ¥1 million with a yearly license fee of around ¥150,000. Additionally, most boats come equipped with solar panels, which eliminates electricity bills. Aside from reducing costs, convenience is another factor. Boats can be moored in or close to central London, giving people easy access to their workplace. There are clearly disadvantages to the houseboat lifestyle, including the lack of space and security. But for many, it is a cost-effective way to live comfortably in one of the world's most expensive cities.

Vocabulary Check

Fill in the blank with words from the word box below. Change the word form if necessary.

1. When Lee saw the traffic accident, he (   ) called the police.

2. I love Hawaii so much that I want to make it my (   ) home.

3. Bob's salary is so low that he (   ) to pay his bills every month.

4. The soccer team lost the game and was (   ) from the competition.

5. My bicycle is (   ) with an electric motor.

immediately	struggle	permanent	equip	eliminate

Reading Comprehension

Answer the following questions.

1. What is the difference between houseboats today and houseboats in the past?

   ____

2. Why are young professionals struggling to pay their monthly bills?

   ____

3. What are some disadvantages of living on a houseboat?

   ____

Writing

TOPIC

- Where would you prefer to live after graduating, an urban area or a rural area?

A *Write your own opinion and give at least one reason.*

____

____

B *Make pairs or groups of 3–4 people and share your ideas with each other.*

Member	Opinion and reason

C *Write down your thoughts with 2 or 3 main points, considering the opinions of your partners (around 60 words).*

____

____

____

____

____

✔ Useful Vocabulary

Category	Examples
Advantages	*lively, restful, nightlife, relaxing, stimulating*
Disadvantages	*remote, stressful, isolated, crowded, expensive*
Other	*cost of living, social life, community spirit, human contact*

UNIT 14

My Italian Town

In this unit, you will learn to ...

- focus on the key vocabulary to understand the main idea of the unit.
- identify key terms relating to cultures and festivals.
- understand the basic usage of inversion.
- express your ideas on cultural events based on information in the tasks and activities.

Warming Up

Choose your own answers to the following questions. Then ask your partner the questions.

1. What yearly event in Japan do you like?
   - ❑ New year's ceremony
   - ❑ Cherry blossom viewing
   - ❑ Obon festival
   - ❑ Other (   )
2. How do you usually spend national holidays?
   - ❑ Hanging out with friends
   - ❑ Traveling to distant places
   - ❑ Returning to your hometown
   - ❑ Staying home and relaxing
3. What festival in the world do you want to go to?
   - ❑ Carnival in Rio de Janeiro
   - ❑ Harbin Ice and Snow Festival
   - ❑ Sydney International Food Festival
   - ❑ La Tomatina in Spain

Watching

WEB動画 DVD CD 2-26

Watch the video and take some notes on what you see and hear. Then, talk about your notes and the topic of the video with your partner.

festival

Vocabulary

CD 2-27

A *Match the words below with the correct explanations (a – f).*

1. celebrate ______
2. procession ______
3. traditional ______
4. incorporate ______
5. performance ______
6. spectacular ______

a. to include someone or something as a member or a part
b. a line of people who are slowly moving in the same direction as part of a ceremony
c. to show that a day or an event is important by doing something special and enjoyable
d. the act of entertaining people through acting, music, dancing, etc.
e. very impressive and magnificent
f. shared customs or beliefs that have remained unchanged for a long time

B *Fill in the blanks with words from Task A. Change the word form if necessary.*

1. Tommy and Gina ( ) their 20th wedding anniversary in Dubai last month.
2. Their live ( ) in Central Park 1998 truly inspired me.
3. Many people walked along the road in the ( ) to mark the religious holiday.

Listening Comprehension

WEB動画 DVD CD 2-26

A *Watch the video again and write T if the statement is true or F if it is false.*

1. Mickela Mallozzi is from the US. ______
2. Mickela's grandmother living in Minturno is a professional dancer. ______
3. Mickela always listens to music to ease her tension and anxiety. ______
4. Thousands of people came to watch the dance from Italy and other countries. ______

B *Which number shows the correct combination of action and the reason for the action during Minturno's festival? Circle the correct number.*

	Reason	What is done
1	to praise a great person in the past	wear folk costumes
2	to mark a religious anniversary	get together with friends and family
3	to celebrate the wheat harvest	parade
4	to remember those who have passed away	dance

Tips on Listening and Speaking

 2-28

Contractions

Contractions, or the short form of two words, are frequently used instead of the full form in spoken English.

1. **I'm** Mickela Mallozzi.
2. I think **we're** ready.

Dictation

 2-29

Listen to the sentences and fill in the blanks.

1. ( ) ( ) ( ) in Italy and is heading to her family's hometown of Minturno.

2. ( ) ( ) two days left.

3. It was amazing. Totally awesome … ( ) ( ) ( ) this.

Retelling

Watch parts of the video again and tell the story of each scene to your partner. You can use the keywords below.

e.g.

Keywords

reaches, climax, last, with

Model

The festival reaches its climax on the last day with a traditional dance.

1.

Keywords

since, in a few days, it, the dancers

2.

Keywords

during, made, Italian culture, as well as

Discussion

Q: *Some historical cities restrict the height and colors of new buildings. Do you agree with these administrative initiatives? Why do you think so? What do you think about your partner's ideas?*

You're right to a certain extent, but …

Oh, you must remember that …

Your ideas	Your partner's ideas

Grammar

Inversion

Normal word order in English is SVO, or subject-verb-object. There are some cases in which the subject and verb are inverted. In other words, they switch position so that the verb comes before the subject. The most common example is in questions, but there are also other situations.

1. **Sentences Starting with Negative Adverbs**
   These include *never, hardly, seldom, no sooner.*
   - Never have I heard such a thing.
   - Seldom have I seen such a great performance.

2. **Conditional Sentences**
   In formal English, inversion sometimes occurs in the conditional part of the sentence.
   - Should he come, please tell him to wait.
   - Had I known, I wouldn't have said anything.

3. **Agreement with "So" and "Neither"**
   - I like pizza. / So do I.
   - I don't like blue cheese. / Neither do I.

Grammar Exercise

Arrange the following words to make full sentences.

1. (worked / had / harder / I), I would have succeeded.

   ____

2. (likes / brother / do / soccer / my / and / so / I).

   ____

3. Seldom (I / have / so / snow / much / seen).

   ____

4. I (don't / sports / play / and / my friend / does / neither).

   ____

5. (will / I / go / there / never) again.

   ____

6. (she / call, / I'll / should / you / let / know).

   ____

Reading

2-30

Harvest festivals are a feature of cultures around the world. Some of them date back thousands of years. The reasons for holding a festival at this important time of the year are not difficult to understand. Harvest season is a time of hard work, when members of a community must work together to collect and store their crops before they go bad. It is therefore only natural that after the hard work is done, people want to come together to celebrate with food and drink, as well as music and dance. But there is also an important religious aspect to such occasions: a harvest festival is a time to give respect and thanks to the gods for the blessings of nature.

Thanksgiving, an important holiday in the United States, has its origins in a harvest festival. Most Americans believe that the celebration dates back to the year 1621. At this time, a group of around 50 English people, who had settled in the town of Plymouth in the state of Massachusetts, celebrated their harvest along with a group of Native Americans. The traditional dishes of a Thanksgiving meal include many foods that were once unique to America, including turkey, cranberries, potatoes, and pumpkin.

Nowadays, Thanksgiving is a day when family members gather, perhaps without giving too much thought to the holiday's origin. But whether the story of how Thanksgiving began is true or not, we can still see that it was a celebration of the harvest.

Vocabulary Check

Fill in the blank with words from the word box below. Change the word form if necessary.

1. The main (　　　　　　　) in my home region are fruits such as apples and pears.
2. Jo is not a (　　　　　　　) person and she does not believe in God.
3. When I graduate, I am going to hold a big party to (　　　　　　　).
4. My grandparents were born in Italy but (　　　　　　　) in Australia.
5. A large crowd (　　　　　　　) in the center of town for a Halloween party yesterday.

settle　celebrate　crop　gather　religious

Reading Comprehension

Answer the following questions.

1. What do people often want to do after working hard to bring in the harvest?

   ____

2. Who celebrated the first Thanksgiving in America?

   ____

3. What is the meaning of Thanksgiving for Americans nowadays?

   ____

Writing

TOPIC

- What kind of traditional event in the city where your university is located would you recommend to people from other places?

A *Write your own opinion and give at least one reason.*

____

____

B *Make pairs or groups of 3–4 people and share your ideas with each other.*

Member	Opinion and reason

C *Write down your thoughts with 2 or 3 main points, considering the opinions of your partners (around 60 words).*

____

____

____

____

____

✔ Useful Vocabulary

Category	Examples
Events	*seasonal festival, music performance, shrine visit, carrying a portable shrine*
Activities	*traditional dancing, parade, procession, taiko drumming*
Other	*food and drink stalls, crowds of people, traditional costume*

UNIT 15 Bengaluru Eco Office

In this unit, you will learn to ...

- focus on the key vocabulary to understand the main idea of the unit.
- identify key terms relating to ecology and the environment.
- understand the basic functions and usage of articles.
- express your opinions on environmental problems based on information in the tasks and activities.

Warming Up

Choose your own answers to the following questions. Then ask your partner the questions.

1. What do you usually do for lunch on weekdays?
   - ❑ Bring your own lunch
   - ❑ Buy food at a convenience store
   - ❑ Eat at the cafeteria
   - ❑ Other (   )
2. How often do you use a reusable bag?
   - ❑ Always
   - ❑ Often
   - ❑ Sometimes
   - ❑ Never
3. Do you take your water bottle with you whenever and wherever you go?
   - ❑ Yes, anytime and anywhere
   - ❑ Only when I go to the university
   - ❑ Only when I work out or play sports
   - ❑ Never

Watching

WEB動画 DVD CD 2-31

Watch the video and take some notes on what you see and hear. Then, talk about your notes and the topic of the video with your partner.

office

Vocabulary

CD 2-32

A *Match the words below with the correct explanations (a – f).*

1. waste ______ a. materials that remain after the useful parts have been removed
2. reduce ______ b. to make something less or smaller
3. environmental ______ c. to eat or drink something
4. conscious ______ d. to decrease something to the lowest possible amount or degree
5. minimize ______ e. aware of or concerned about something
6. consume ______ f. relating to the natural conditions on Earth

B *Fill in the blanks with words from Task A. Change the word form if necessary.*

1. My parents are trying to avoid (   ) salt and sugar as much as possible.
2. Each of us should be environmentally (   ) when we buy products.
3. One of the most serious issues with nuclear power plants is the disposal of radioactive (   ).

Listening Comprehension

WEB動画 DVD CD 2-31

A *Watch the video again and write T if the statement is true or F if it is false.*

1. Bengaluru, one of the biggest cities in India, faces the problem of a large amount of garbage. ______
2. The Graffiti staff members never use air conditioners because they can keep the room temperature comfortable by opening the windows. ______
3. The Graffiti staff members sometimes eat meat and fish. ______
4. The people at Graffiti cook for themselves at their office, so they do not eat out for lunch. ______

B ***What materials does Graffiti use to reduce waste in the video? Join the correct combinations using lines.***

A. various materials	•	•	**1.** notebooks
B. kitchen waste	•	•	**2.** plant food
C. waste paper	•	•	**3.** comfortable and stylish chairs
D. old tires	•	•	**4.** appealing decorations

Tips on Listening and Speaking

 2-33

Dropping [ð] (Weak Form)

The [ð] sound in words (e.g., *the, this, that, they, them, their*) is often unvoiced unless these words appear at the beginning of a sentence.

1. From **th**e outside, it looks like any other office.
2. The first is **th**at **th**ey don't have any air conditioning.

Dictation

 2-34

Listen to the sentences and fill in the blanks.

1. But inside, you'll find a group of creative people who care (　　　　　) (　　　　　) (　　　　　).

2. They cook (　　　　　) (　　　　　) (　　　　　) (　　　　　) office kitchen, as it saves on a lot of plastic waste that comes with food packaging.

3. We cook our lunch, we eat together, (　　　　　) (　　　　　) (　　　　　) (　　　　　) together.

Retelling

Watch parts of the video again and tell the story of each scene to your partner. You can use the keywords below.

e.g.

Keywords

Graffiti Collaborative, group, eco-friendly, protect

Model

Graffiti Collaborative is a group that takes eco-friendly action to protect the environment.

1.

Keywords

leftover food, grow, vegetables, in their office

2.

Keywords

any office, care, environment, simple and easy way

Discussion

Q: ***Do you agree all university classes should go paperless to help the environment? Why do you think so? What do you think about your partner's ideas?***

Hmm … it depends.

OK, let's go over pros and cons.

Your ideas	Your partner's ideas

Grammar

Articles

There are three types of article in English, the definite article (*the*), the indefinite article (*a, an*), and the zero article.

1. **Indefinite Article**
This is used with any example of a thing, not a specific example.
    - A car stopped at a traffic signal.
    - My friend has a dog.

2. **Definite Article**
This is used with something that is specific, known, or previously mentioned.
    - The car parked outside is mine.
    - There's the man we saw yesterday.

3. **Zero Article**
This is used to refer to things in general, particularly plural and uncountable nouns.
    - Dogs are loyal animals.
    - I don't eat meat.

Grammar Exercise

Arrange the following words to make full sentences.

1. (common / are / pigeons / birds / in) cities.
____
2. (I / the / bought / jacket / is / in / my) closet.
____
3. (a / I / online / book / bought) today.
____
4. (the / member / my / favorite / is / band / of) the singer.
____
5. (coffee / I / to / drink / with / like) breakfast.
____
6. (I / armchair / an / have / my / in) room.
____

Reading

2-35

NASA, the US space agency, recently reported that global temperatures reached the highest levels since record keeping began in the mid-1800s. It is clear that serious efforts must be made to tackle climate change. The responsibility to do so lies not only with governments and individuals, but also with companies, which have a duty to conduct their economic activities in a way that benefits society.

Some large companies are committed to recycling and reusing materials. One such company is McDonalds, which recycles toys that come with its Happy Meals. If customers have toys that they no longer use, they can put them in a collection box at a McDonalds store. They will then be recycled to produce trays for use in the stores. Another is Uniqlo, Japan's largest clothing retailer, which has a program to collect used clothing. Customers can bring items they no longer wear to a store, and Uniqlo will send them to places such as refugee camps. Another example is Coca-Cola. The company is making great progress in recycling PET bottles and it also plans to stop using raw materials derived from petroleum by 2030.

In Japan, waste generated by businesses accounts for around 30 percent of the total amount. Companies can help society as a whole, and improve their public image at the same time, if they make sincere efforts to apply the three Rs – reduce, reuse, recycle – in their business activities.

Vocabulary Check

Fill in the blank with words from the word box below. Change the word form if necessary.

1. As a parent, I have ( ) for the welfare of my children.

2. My company is ( ) to helping the local community.

3. Many ( ) experienced a fall in sales during the COVID-19 pandemic.

4. As a result of the war, many ( ) tried to find a new home.

5. Oil is the main raw ( ) used to make plastic.

committed	retailer	responsibility	material	refugee

Reading Comprehension

Answer the following questions.

1. In addition to governments, who is responsible for making efforts to tackle climate change?

   ____

2. What does McDonalds do with unwanted toys from Happy Meals?

   ____

3. In terms of the environment, what do the "three R's" stand for?

   ____

TOPIC

• What is the most serious environmental problem?

A *Write your own opinion and give at least one reason.*

____

____

B *Make pairs or groups of 3–4 people and share your ideas with each other.*

Member	Opinion and reason

C *Write down your thoughts with 2 or 3 main points, considering the opinions of your partners (around 60 words).*

____

____

____

____

____

✔ Useful Vocabulary

Category	Examples
Problems	*climate change, ocean plastic, air/water pollution, species extinction*
Solutions	*geoengineering, renewable energy, electric vehicles, cutting consumption*
Other	*biodiversity, carbon footprint, fossil fuels*

Appendix

Useful Expressions for Discussions

Starting a discussion

☐ Today, we are going to discuss …

☐ Today's topic is …

☐ Let's begin with …

Giving your opinion

☐ I think that … because …

☐ In my opinion, …

☐ I personally feel …

☐ As far as I am concerned, …

☐ I'm not sure, but perhaps …

☐ I strongly believe that …

☐ There's no doubt in my mind that …

Reacting

☐ I see.

☐ Really?

☐ That's interesting.

☐ Is that right?

☐ I didn't know that.

☐ Go on, please.

Asking for an opinion

☐ What do you think?

☐ What's your view?

☐ Do you agree?

☐ How about you?

- [ ] Could you tell me …?
- [ ] Could I have your opinion?

Agreeing

- [ ] I think so, too.
- [ ] I totally agree.
- [ ] I agree with you.
- [ ] That's a good point.
- [ ] I see what you mean.
- [ ] That is exactly what I think.
- [ ] Exactly.
- [ ] That makes sense.

Partially agreeing

- [ ] Yes, perhaps, but …
- [ ] That may be true, but …
- [ ] I suppose so. However, …
- [ ] You're right to a certain extent, but …
- [ ] Hmm …, it depends.

Disagreeing

- [ ] I don't think so.
- [ ] I disagree with you.
- [ ] I am afraid that is not quite true.
- [ ] I'm sorry, I really can't accept your idea.
- [ ] I take a different view.
- [ ] Actually, I think …

- ☐ It is interesting, but …
- ☐ I see your point, but …

Not sure

- ☐ I'm not really sure about that.
- ☐ I have never thought about that before.
- ☐ I haven't made up my mind yet.
- ☐ Um … let me think about it.
- ☐ That's a difficult question.
- ☐ It's hard to say.

Asking for a clarification

- ☐ Excuse me?
- ☐ Do you mean …?
- ☐ Did you say that …?
- ☐ I think you said …, right?
- ☐ What exactly does that mean?
- ☐ Sorry, I didn't catch that.

Asking for explanations

- ☐ Could you explain …?
- ☐ Could you give me an example?
- ☐ Could you tell me a bit more about that?
- ☐ Could you tell me why?

Listing points

- [ ] First (of all), … Second, … Third, …
- [ ] In addition, …
- [ ] Besides that, …
- [ ] Moreover, …
- [ ] Furthermore, …
- [ ] Lastly, …

Showing importance

- [ ] The key point is …
- [ ] The main idea is …
- [ ] The most important thing is …
- [ ] What I want to say is …

Referring to a source

- [ ] I read/heard that …
- [ ] According to the article, …
- [ ] As … shows, …
- [ ] The researcher argues that …

Giving examples or explanations

- [ ] The main problem is …
- [ ] Furthermore, …
- [ ] For example, …
- [ ] In cases such as …
- [ ] In fact,
- [ ] … like …

- [ ] …, including …
- [ ] Oh, you must remember that …

Giving a cause and effect

- [ ] The reason why … is …
- [ ] … because …
- [ ] Due to …
- [ ] Since …,
- [ ] This is why …
- [ ] Therefore
- [ ] As a result, …
- [ ] Thus, …

Describing both sides of an argument

- [ ] OK, let's go over pros and cons.
- [ ] What are the pros and cons of …
- [ ] What are advantages/disadvantages of …
- [ ] The advantages/disadvantages are …
- [ ] On the one hand …, but the other hand …
- [ ] Some people think/say that …but others think/say that …

Comparing and contrasting

- [ ] Also, …
- [ ] Likewise, …
- [ ] In contrast, …
- [ ] …, but …
- [ ] …, while

☐ A is the same as B.

☐ A is similar to B.

☐ A is different from B.

Interrupting

☐ Sorry to interrupt, but …

☐ Excuse me, but could I ask something?

☐ May I add something at this point?

Restating

☐ What I mean is …

☐ What I'm trying to say is …

☐ In other words, …

☐ That is …

Summarizing or concluding

☐ To sum up, …

☐ We pointed out that …

☐ Let me summarize the key points of our opinion.

☐ Let's wrap up our discussion.

Web動画のご案内　StreamLine

本テキストの映像は、オンラインでのストリーミング再生になります。下記URLよりご利用ください。なお**有効期限は、はじめてログインした時点から1年半**です。

http://st.seibido.co.jp

1

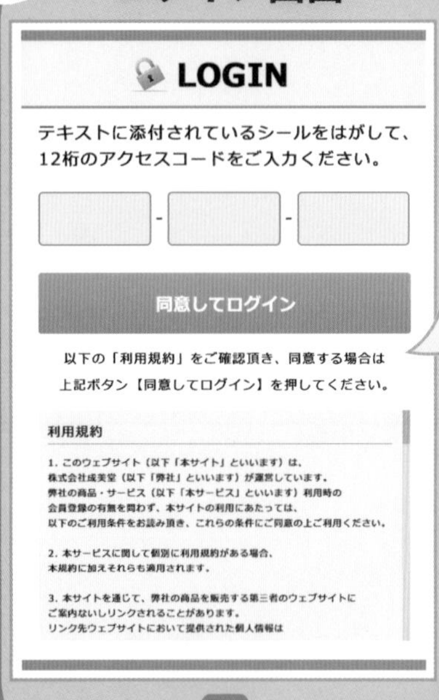

巻末に添付されているシールをはがして、アクセスコードをご入力ください。

2

メニュー画面

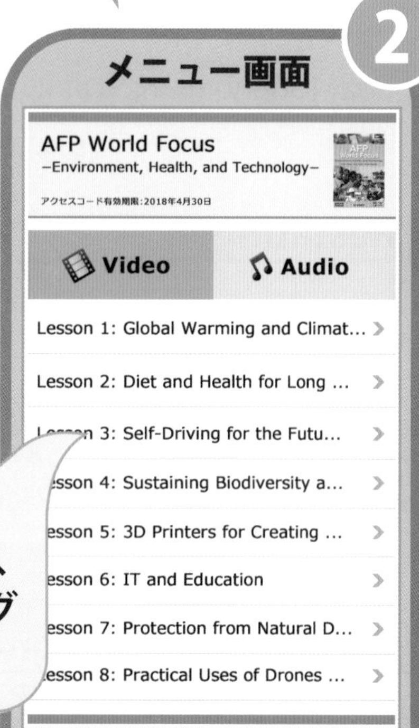

「Video」または「Audio」を選択すると、それぞれストリーミング再生ができます。

3

再生画面

Lesson 2:
Diet and Health for Long Lives
食習慣：長生きのためのスーパーフードを探す

推奨動作環境

【PC OS】
Windows 7~ / Mac 10.8~

【Mobile OS】
iOS / Android ※Android の場合は4.x~が推奨

【Desktop ブラウザ】
Internet Explorer 9~ / Firefox / Chrome / Safari

Global Gate TESTUDY のご案内

STUDY 学習内容

教科書の学習をWeb上に再現しております。
リアルタイムで学習状況を確認することができます。

教科書タスク	TESTUDY 学習形式
Warming Up	多肢選択問題
Watching	動画再生
Vocabulary	タイピング問題
Listening Comprehension	動画再生および多肢選択問題など
Dictation	タイピング問題
Retelling	動画再生および自由記入フォーム
Discussion	自由記入フォーム
Grammar Exercise	語句整序問題
Reading	本文掲載
Vocabulary Check	タイピング問題
Reading Comprehension	自由記入フォーム
Writing	自由記入フォーム

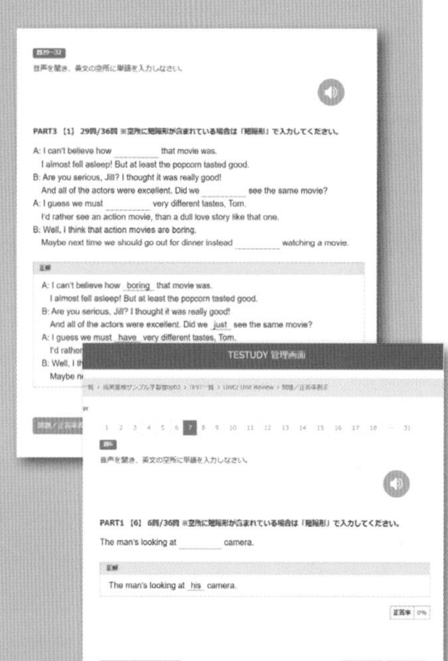

REVIEW 学習内容

授業の復習に活用することができます。

教科書タスク	TESTUDY 学習形式
Vocabulary	多肢選択問題
Tips on Listening and Speaking	音声認識学習
Dictation	タイピング問題
Grammar Exercise	語句整序問題

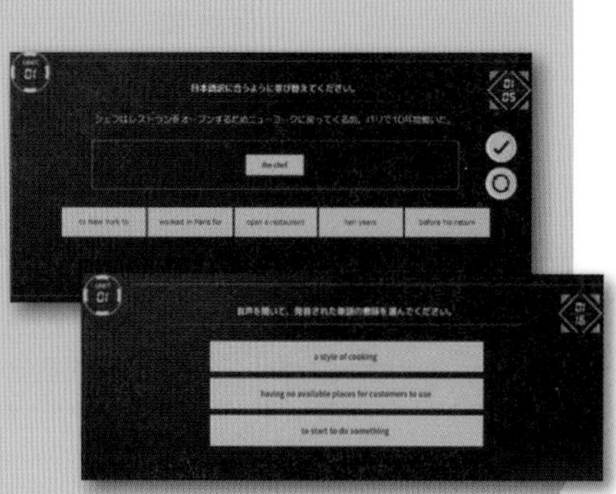

※教員の指示に従って学習・受験してください。

著者

和田 あずさ　（宮城教育大学 講師）
Bill Benfield　（株式会社成美堂）
森田 彰　（早稲田大学 教授）

TEXT PRODUCTION STAFF

edited by　編集
Takashi Kudo　工藤 隆志
Eiichi Tamura　田村 栄一
Mitsugu Shishido　宍戸 貢
Hiroshi Yoshizuka　吉塚 弘

cover design by　表紙デザイン
Nobuyoshi Fujino　藤野 伸芳

DTP by　DTP
ALIUS (Hiroyuki Kinouchi)　アリウス（木野内 宏行）

CD PRODUCTION STAFF

recorded by　吹き込み者
Dominic Allen (AmE)　ドミニク・アレン（アメリカ英語）
Howard Colefield (AmE)　ハワード・コールフィルド（アメリカ英語）
Rachel Walzer (AmE)　レイチェル・ワルザー（アメリカ英語）
Karen Headrich (AmE)　カレン・ヘドリック（アメリカ英語）

Global Gate Intermediate
-Video-based Four Skills Training-

2024年1月20日　初版発行
2024年2月15日　第2刷発行

著　者　和田 あずさ　Bill Benfield
森田 彰

発 行 者　佐野 英一郎

発 行 所　株式会社 成 美 堂
〒101-0052　東京都千代田区神田小川町3-22
TEL 03-3291-2261　FAX 03-3293-5490
https://www.seibido.co.jp

印 刷・製 本　三美印刷株式会社

ISBN 978-4-7919-7282-1　Printed in Japan